T5-BAE-897

SOVIET FOREIGN ECONOMIC POLICY UNDER PERESTROIKA

SOVIET FOREIGN ECONOMIC POLICY UNDER PERESTROIKA

Leonard Geron

PUBLISHED IN NORTH AMERICA FOR

THE ROYAL INSTITUTE OF INTERNATIONAL AFFAIRS

COUNCIL ON FOREIGN RELATIONS PRESS
• NEW YORK •

Chatham House Papers

Soviet Foreign Policy Programme Director: Neil Malcolm

The Royal Institute of International Affairs, at Chatham House in London, has provided an impartial forum for discussion and debate on current international issues for 70 years. Its resident research fellows, specialized information resources, and range of publications, conferences, and meetings span the fields of international politics, economics, and security. The Institute is independent of government.

Chatham House Papers are short monographs on current policy problems which have been commissioned by the RIIA. In preparing the papers, authors are advised by a study group of experts convened by the RIIA, and publication of a paper indicates that the Institute regards it as an authoritative contribution to the public debate. The Institute does not, however, hold opinions of its own; the views expressed in this publication are the responsibility of the author.

Copyright © 1990 by Royal Institute of International Affairs.
All rights reserved.
Printed in the United States of America.

This book may not be reproduced, in whole or in part, in any form (beyond that copying permitted by Sections 107 and 108 of the U.S. Copyright Law and excerpts by reviewers for the public press), without written permission from the publishers. For information, write Publications Office, Council on Foreign Relations®, 58 East 68th Street, New York, NY 10021.

Library of Congress Cataloguing-in-Publication Data

Geron, Leonard.
    Soviet foreign economic policy under perestroika /Leonard Geron.
        p.   cm.—(Chatham House papers)
    Includes bibliographical references.
    ISBN 0-87609-094-3 : $14.95
    1. Soviet Union—Foreign economic relations. 2. Perestroika.
    I. Title II. Series: Chatham House papers (Unnumbered)
    HF1557.G48 1991
    337.47—dc20
                                                        90-25250
                                                            CIP

91   92   93   94   95   96   97   PB   10   9   8   7   6   5   4   3   2   1

337.47
G377s

For Daniel and Tal

CONTENTS

ACKNOWLEDGMENTS

This paper could not have been written without the advice, encouragement and support of many institutions, experts, colleagues and friends. It is impossible to name all those to whom I am indebted, but, above all, my thanks go to Dr Neil Malcolm and Dr Alex Pravda, the present and the past Directors of the Soviet Foreign Policy Programme at the Royal Institute of International Affairs. I would also like to thank Dr Guzel Anulova (IMEMO), Dr Igor Artemiev (IMEMO), Dr Judy Batt (RIIA), Dr Sergei Chebanov (IMEMO), Maurice Childs (CBI), Richard J. Cole (Midland Bank, Moscow Office), Dr Martin Dangerfield, Nikolai Denisenko (State Foreign Economic Commission of the Council of Ministers of the USSR), David Fligelis (*Tiesa*), Kester George (DTI), Vasili Gerasimov (JV Mezhnumizmatika), Dr Brigitte Granville (RIIA), Rimvydas Jasinavichius (the Government of Lithuania), Michael Johnson (DTI), Michael Kaser (St Antony's College, Oxford), Professor Efim Khesin (IMEMO), Raimondas Kutra (The Bank for Foreign Economic Affairs of the USSR, The Lithuanian Republican Bank), Aleksandr Levinsonas (Institute of Economics, Lithuania), Rimgaudas Malishauskas (Ministry of Foreign Affairs, Lithuania), Vladislovas Mikuchauskas (Ministry of Foreign Affairs, Lithuania), Alfonsas Mozuras (Gosplan, Lithuania), Jeremy Russell (Shell), Dr Gerald Segal (RIIA), Arvydas Sekmokas (JV Baltic Amadeus), Professor Yuri Shishkov (IMEMO), Dr Andrei Sizov (IMEMO), Dr

Acknowledgments

Victor Spandarian (ISKAN), Frank Trippett (US Embassy, London), Mark S. Vecchio (Coudert Brothers, Moscow Office), Richard Ware (Bank of England), Nicolas L. M. Wolfers (Midland Bank), Juozas Zalatorius (JV Baltic Amadeus), and Algirdas Yurgelevichius (Gosplan, Lithuania). Needless to say, the opinions expressed in the paper are my responsibility, as are any mistakes or omissions.

My thanks go also to the Institute's staff for their support, primarily to the programme assistant Shyama Iyer, and to Pauline Wickham and Hannah Doe in the Publications Department. Most of all I would like to thank my wife Ahouva and sons Daniel and Tal for their love, patience and understanding.

The paper was written during my stay at the Royal Institute of International Affairs from mid-1989 to mid-1990, and thus does not cover in detail the events of the second half of 1990.

This paper would not have been possible without the generous funding provided by the ESRC (grant no. E 00 22 2011).

September 1990   Leonard Geron

1
INTRODUCTION

Changes in foreign economic policy are an integral part of the overall economic and political reform initiated in the USSR by Mikhail Gorbachev. Indeed, the process of decentralization and demonopolization of foreign economic management is a cornerstone of that reform. Starting in 1986, the process of foreign economic reform had resulted by mid-1990 in there being over 15,000 Soviet enterprises and organizations registered as direct participants in foreign economic relations. To this number could be added over 200,000 newly created cooperatives, with the right to participate in foreign trade. By July 1990 over 1,800 joint ventures with foreign, mainly Western, companies were registered in the USSR, although only 15%-20% of them had actually started to operate. These changes signify the most profound reform of Soviet external economic relations since the New Economic Policy (NEP) of the 1920s. Moreover, whereas the NEP period was characterized by the leadership as a forced tactical retreat, the contemporary process of perestroika constitutes a strategic and probably irreversible political and economic reorientation.

This book cannot claim to be a comprehensive survey. Rather, it analyses the main features of Soviet foreign economic policy under perestroika and connects them with the broader process of reform. In the following chapters, I shall briefly outline the history of foreign economic policy since the creation of the Soviet state, the organiza-

1

tion of Soviet foreign trade and the debates surrounding it, its structure and patterns, the policy of joint ventures, Soviet policy towards the international economic organizations, and the future of the reform. Foreign economic relations have in the past been a closely guarded monopoly of the state. We shall consider how far the current changes have encroached on this monopoly and whether we are witnessing a forced tactical retreat or a strategic change of course. I shall argue that, though forced, the present changes are long-lasting and irreversible.

In Chapter 2, I shall consider the changes which have been introduced in legislation governing trade with other countries, as well as the evolving organizational mechanism of foreign trade and its shift away from being highly centralized and monopolistic. I shall also consider likely future developments. It will be argued that the legislation so far has been radical by comparison with that of the past, but is nevertheless incomplete and not radical enough to be effective under present conditions. I shall look at the different views expressed in the Soviet Union about the economic opening-up to the outside world. The debate revolves around the issue of Soviet involvement in and interdependence with the world economy. I shall present the arguments put forward by both conservatives and liberals and see where they clash.

The patterns of Soviet foreign trade will be discussed in Chapter 3. These have not changed in the past five years and are unlikely to be substantially altered for at least another decade. This is true of the geographical pattern of trade both with the developed Western countries and with the other members of the CMEA (Council for Mutual Economic Assistance). The CMEA may disintegrate, but its members' trade with the USSR will change only slightly, even though it will be conducted on a hard-currency basis. After decades of consistent growth, Soviet foreign trade turnover has dropped since 1985 and still has not reached the pre-perestroika level. I shall consider the causes and the trends of that development and how they may change in the future.

In Chapter 4, I shall explore the development of the joint venture policy and its potential. Arguably, this is the most spectacular change in Soviet foreign economic policy, which has a direct influence on the domestic economy, providing an avenue for direct foreign investment in the USSR. The policy of joint ventures and special economic zones is controversial in the USSR. Some argue that it leads to the 'selling out of Mother Russia to foreigners', while others see it almost as a panacea for the ills of Soviet economy. Whose arguments prevail to date? How successful has this policy been so far in attracting foreign investment and cooperation? I shall conclude that, although it is marred by excessive bureaucracy and hindered by objective economic difficulties, the joint venture policy is reasonably promising.

In Chapter 5, I shall examine changes in Soviet policy towards international economic organizations, such as the General Agreement on Tariffs and Trade (GATT), the International Monetary Fund (IMF), the World Bank and the European Community (EC), and ask what the Western response to these changes is likely to be. A notable shift in the policies of both the USSR and the West has already occurred: the USSR has been granted observer status by GATT and has established diplomatic relations with the EC. What would be the costs and benefits of closer involvement both for the Soviet Union and for the international community? In spite of its domestic economic difficulties, the Soviet Union is a major provider of economic and military aid to Third World countries and to its strategic and political allies. What is the Soviet role in international organizations going to be? Will it be a donor nation or a borrower? The Western countries would like to support the process of perestroika, not just through arms reductions and the reduction of the CoCom (Coordinating Committee for East-West trade) restrictions, but also by providing tangible financial aid to the USSR. What then would be the necessary conditions for such aid? I argue that the USSR will have substantially to restructure its domestic economy along market economy lines, to introduce far-reaching political reforms, and to reduce its role as a global military power.

Finally, in Chapter 6, I shall consider the relationship between domestic economic and foreign economic policy. What should be the West's response to the Soviet reforms? Is there a case merely for moral support, or for financial and technological support and cooperation, or for a mix of these? I shall argue here that the most effective Western support for perestroika would be in the form of technological and educational cooperation, in joint ventures and in closer cooperation within the frameworks of international economic organizations. Direct financial assistance, when it is offered, should be mainly project-related. In a still highly centralized, bureaucratized and horrendously inefficient system, large unconditional credits would be wasteful and counter-productive. The USSR must transform itself from within, using its own strengths and advantages. The outside world can facilitate this transition, but it cannot solve the problems of the Soviet Union.

The changing organization of foreign trade

The first Soviet government (formed in November 1917) included a People's Commissariat of Trade and Industry, which dealt initially with industry, trade and merchant marine. Very soon after its creation, although retaining its original name,* the Commissariat began to deal exclusively with the organization of foreign trade. In charge of the whole economy was the Supreme Council of the National Economy, which Lenin described as 'the fighting organ for the struggle with the capitalists and the landlords in the economic sphere, just as Sovnarkom [Council of People's Commissars] is in politics'.[1] The Soviet regime endorsed the general principle laid down by the *Communist Manifesto* of centralization of economic activity in a proletarian state. Although it did not deal in particular with foreign trade, the *Manifesto* specifically prescribed the need for centralization of all instruments of production, credit, means of communication and transport.[2] Indeed, the Bolsheviks regarded foreign trade as one of the key areas to be brought firmly under state control. As E. H. Carr expressed it, 'Soviet foreign policy was first conceived as a defensive action,'[3] a defensive action against the *economic power* of foreign capital.

In the period 1917–20 Soviet foreign trade was virtually non-existent. Thus, whereas in 1913 the volume of trade was R10.1bn (at 1950 prices), it dropped to a mere R11.3m in 1919. It started to

* On 11 June 1920, it was renamed the People's Commissariat of Foreign Trade, and headed by Leonid Krasin.

recover only after the Allies resolved in January 1920 to lift the blockade imposed in 1918 following the Soviet-German treaty of Brest-Litovsk. Trade turnover increased considerably during the more liberal NEP period following 1921. After Stalin abandoned NEP, trade volume – having peaked in 1930 (at R7.3bn) – started to fall during the following decade, decreasing to R1.2bn by 1939.

At no time after 1917 was Soviet foreign trade organized on a market basis. It was characterized by a limited degree of decentralization, however, during the period of NEP in the 1920s. The party recognized at that time that there was a need to allow direct ties between Soviet industry and foreign markets, while preserving the foreign trade monopoly. Regional cooperatives, state industrial associations, joint-stock companies and other large economic agencies, as well as private persons, were permitted to carry out export and import operations. However, their freedom of action was limited: each transaction had to be separately authorized by the People's Commissariat of Foreign Trade,[4] which in the 1920s was thus temporarily transformed from an operational into a regulatory body. It was given the tasks of issuing export and import permits, of creating a system for supervision and control of the foreign trade organizations, and of introducing customs duties. A policy of concessions and of cooperation with Western partners emerged quite soon after the Revolution. From the late 1920s to the 1980s, however, no non-government entities or foreign-owned concessions engaged in foreign trade.

World War II transformed international economic relations. The victors set about creating a more orderly and stable world. The Bretton Woods system of international economic management established the rules for commercial and financial relations between 44 states. The Soviet Union participated in the work of the conference, but at the last moment refused to join the new economic system. It did not ratify the agreement, and declined membership in its agencies. It also refused to accept American aid offered under the Marshall Plan. Instead, in January 1949, the Soviet Union, together with its satellite countries in Eastern Europe, set up the CMEA. By the end of the 1940s, two separate economic systems had emerged. The world had become bipolar in economic as well as in political terms. This world was seen by leaders in East and West not simply as one of competition, but as one of zero-sum struggle (in which each gain for one side represented a loss for the other). In 1952 Stalin explained that 'the economic consequence of the existence of two opposite camps was that the single, all-embracing world market disintegrated, so that now we have two parallel world markets, also confronting one another'.[5]

The Soviet Union's foreign trade expanded after World War II and until 1985. Its share in world trade, however, remained below that held by Russia in 1913. Raw materials constituted the bulk of Soviet exports (some 80% of the total), while the larger part of imports consisted of machinery and equipment. The technological level of most of Soviet industry remained inferior to that achieved in the West. In the 1960s and 1970s it became clear that European and American technology would have to be used on a large scale in order to achieve the kind of intensive industrial growth needed to modernize the domestic economy and shift the export structure away from primary products. By the 1980s there was a widespread consensus of informed opinion that far-reaching change was needed. But it took a combination of major setbacks in military, political and economic competition with the West to provoke a fundamental change embracing domestic and external economic policy and associated political and social reforms. A few words must be said about the circumstances that contributed to the overall change of course and about its nature.

Perestroika and foreign trade

Perestroika represents a wide-ranging and complex reform which aims to transform the Soviet Union's economy and society. Foreign economic policy has itself to be reformed and it is expected to facilitate the achievement of the reform in other spheres, especially in the domestic economy. Perestroika and foreign trade are thus inseparable. Soviet industrial development strategy since the 1920s had put the emphasis overwhelmingly on meeting quantitative output targets. Quality and efficiency have been of less concern. After several decades of following this 'extensive growth' path,

Soviet industry was squandering huge amounts of natural resources. The American economist Marshal I. Goldman demonstrated in 1988 that Soviet factories required three times more coal to produce a dollar's worth of gross domestic product than did West German factories.[6] One Soviet author has estimated that the amount of iron and energy needed to produce a given level of industrial output exceed the Western averages by 1.7 times and 1.53 times respectively.[7] The experience of the post-Stalin decades seems to show that it was beyond the capacity of the existing centralized economic system to execute the necessary change of course in the direction of intensive growth and high quality.

The sectoral pattern was distorted towards heavy industry and military production, while the production of consumer goods and especially of high-technology consumer products was seen as being of secondary importance. Inflationary pressures mounted, the population's income grew and involuntary savings accumulated, while scarcities of consumer goods worsened. Those goods that the under-resourced and monopolized light-industrial sector could produce had little appeal to the public. As a result cash incentives and bonuses lost their potency. Labour productivity remained at an obstinately low level. Agriculture, in particular, suffered from neglect and mismanagement. It has been reported that as much as 20% of Soviet crops, 60%-70% of fruit and vegetables, and 10% of meat are lost, spoil or rot in the field each year.[8] The practice became established of spending huge sums on food subsidies and large amounts of precious hard currency on agricultural imports. According to data from the UN's Food and Agricultural Organization (FAO), from 1971 to 1988 the Soviet Union purchased from abroad 483 million tonnes of grain at a cost of $70bn. *Izvestiya* commented recently that the USSR had begun to depend on imports 'in the same way as a drug addict depends on the needle'.[9]

The weaknesses of the Soviet economy were thus drawing it inexorably into greater dependence on the outside world. Stalin's vision of 'two parallel' world economies confronting each other was being discredited, too, in the more advanced sectors. Here, Soviet authors began to note, the 'Scientific-Technological Revolution' was widening the front of technical progress and deepening international specialization. The old autarkic policy was becoming more and more difficult to sustain. When attempts were made to modify it and to participate more wholeheartedly in the international division of labour, they were crippled by the rigidities of the state monopoly system. Enterprises wishing to import faced endless delays and restrictions, while those that might have been able to sell abroad had little incentive to do so, since the hard currency earned would flow directly into the state budget. The Soviet Union did not participate in international economic organizations such as GATT, the World Bank and the IMF, or in their agreements. The NATO countries, along with Japan, restricted technology transfers to the Eastern bloc through the CoCom regulations. This embargo was informally adhered to by the other developed Western countries.

As the climate of East-West relations deteriorated at the end of the 1970s, it became painfully clear that existing Soviet internal and foreign policies not only tended to perpetuate confrontation, but rendered the USSR less and less competitive in the struggle. The war in Afghanistan, and the outcome of the Israeli-Syrian clash in the Lebanon in 1982, demonstrated the country's relative military and technological weakness. The subsequent challenge of President Reagan's Strategic Defense Initiative (SDI) drew attention to this weakness in the most urgent way. In domestic affairs, too, there were increasingly obvious signs – corruption, demoralization, waste and ecological deterioration – that the neo-Stalinist 'command-administrative system' had exhausted its usefulness.

The new generation of leaders who came to power in Moscow in 1985 set about promoting a comprehensive transformation in which the idea of conflict – with the 'class enemy' internally and with 'imperialism' externally – was replaced as a guiding principle by ideas of compromise, cooperation and a balance of interests. They moved to bring about a demilitarization of external relations and a corresponding demilitarization of the economy. Unlike previous partial decentralizers, such as Lenin and Khrushchev, Gorbachev genuinely sought to devolve initiative and the power of decision-making to the lower levels of organization in the economy, reserving for the central administration only regulatory and general supervisory powers. Perestroika was not described as a forced retreat, unlike the NEP of the 1920s. In 1988, Vadim Medvedev, Party Ideology Secretary, stated that the new policy was 'a real advance forward ... from the viewpoint of social maturity'.[10] By 1990 the government appeared more and more to be aiming for convergence with Western political and economic patterns, to the extent of dismantling the one-party system and abandoning its insistence on public ownership of productive assets.

Official statements on foreign affairs have begun to emphasize the mutual nature of security and the interconnectedness of a *single* world economy. They express a tolerance of variety – 'the states and peoples of the earth are very different, and it is actually good that they are so', wrote Gorbachev in 1987[11] – and refer to the overarching nature of 'all-human values', on the basis of which all nations are urged to combine their forces in order to solve the global problems of ecological disaster, economic dislocation, famine, disease and terrorism. The political and ideological context in which the Soviet economy is being opened up to greater international cooperation is quite different from that which existed in the 1920s. Unlike Lenin, writes Goldman, 'Gorbachev has not justified re-admitting foreign investors with the notion that two steps forward require a step backward. For Gorbachev this is entirely a step forward.'[12]

There is no denying the commitment of the Soviet leadership to the integration of their country into the world economy. It is when we come to estimate their chances of success that doubts arise. They have inherited an outdated industrial base, an underdeveloped infrastructure, and a population that has yet to adapt to the values of the market economy. Stubborn resistance from officials at the middle level has slowed the pace of domestic economic reform, which has indeed barely started. The old command system has begun to crumble, while the market system that is to replace it is still unformed. The upheavals inseparable from radical change have already undermined the government's popularity to a damaging extent and have provoked serious labour unrest. Prospective Western partners are still cautious, and governments are reluctant to lift restrictions on technology transfer too swiftly.

Prospects for the future will be discussed in more detail in Chapter 6. Meanwhile, it is worth commenting that Russian and Soviet history has seen several periods of change and radical reform – under Peter the Great at the beginning of the eighteenth century, under Alexander II in the 1860s and under Stolypin in the years following defeat in the Russo-Japanese war of 1904–5 – all followed by counter-reform, and then by stagnation and decline.[13] Each time the spiral turns, however, conditions inside the country and in the international environment have changed. The progress Gorbachev has made so far is a demonstration, for instance, of the increased weight and influence of the Westernized, educated part of Soviet society. As the spokesmen of this segment never tire of pointing out, the world economy is becoming increasingly integrated, and interdependence is becoming more and more evident in different spheres of international relations. Factors such as these suggest some grounds for the optimistic belief that a drastic reversal of reform is not inevitable and that the changes outlined in later chapters mark the beginnings of a permanent shift in the pattern of Soviet economic relations with the outside world.

2
THE INSTITUTIONAL AND LEGISLATIVE BASE

From the end of the 1920s until 1987 Soviet foreign trade remained a state monopoly. More than 90% of foreign trade turnover was managed by the subsidiaries of just one agency – the Ministry of Foreign Trade. In the pre-perestroika Soviet Union most of the 'foreign trade associations' that formed part of the Ministry of Foreign Trade specialized in trade in certain goods or commodities; thus, for example, Avtoexport traded in motor vehicles and Aviaexport in aircraft. Some engaged both in exports and in imports, others undertook only one or the other, and others still provided foreign trade services such as transport and advertising.

A minority of foreign trade associations were subordinated to other central agencies, for example to the State Committee for Foreign Economic Relations (GKES), or the State Committee for Science and Technology (GKNT).

Plans for foreign economic activity had to be submitted to the State Planning Committee (Gosplan), the State Committee for Material Technical Supplies (Gossnab), the Ministry of Finance, the Ministry of Foreign Trade and the USSR Council of Ministers. This was a long and complicated process involving a vast bureaucracy.[1] The whole system was highly centralized and overmanned. Gosplan, as the chief agency for economic planning in the USSR, had the task of setting the export and import targets for each and every item, for every single factory or enterprise. The most important plan was that for export, since foreign-currency receipts depended on it. This, however, should not be taken as evidence that the Soviet economy was export-led. In fact it was the size of the country's import requirements which dictated the amount that had to be exported in a particular year.

Relations with the CMEA

Permission for direct economic ties with the CMEA countries by industrial, rather than specifically foreign trade, agencies was granted under Leonid Brezhnev in August 1977, almost a decade before direct links with Western countries were allowed.[2] The relevant resolution granted ministries and departments the right to conclude agreements – with parallel institutions in the CMEA countries – on the exchange of goods that fell under their competence. The exchange, which could be conducted on a direct basis or through the Vneshpromtekhobmen association (part of Gossnab),* was limited to counter-trade only. A small financial incentive – a commission of 4% in transferable roubles from their total revenues – was the only reward to departments and ministries that followed this procedure. Vneshpromtekhobmen, too, was granted the right to trade directly with the CMEA countries, when approached by any of them, in above-plan goods.

A further decentralization of foreign trade institutions got under way on 9 July 1981, when the Council of Ministers resolved to grant sectoral branch ministries, and, with their permission, subordinate associations and enterprises, the right to establish direct contacts with their counterparts in the CMEA member countries. The same decree granted certain rights of direct cooperation on scientific and technical matters between the CMEA member countries and the industrial association Vneshtekhnika, a subsidiary of the GKNT,

* The All-Union Association (VO) Vneshpromtekhobmen (literally, 'association for external exchange in industry and technology') was set up on 15 September 1975 as a subsidiary of Gossnab for the purpose of the operational management of the exchange of goods between the USSR and the CMEA member countries (see SZ SSSR, vol. 9, pp. 133–4). The association had only operational responsibilities and was required to coordinate its trade transactions through the Ministry of Foreign Trade.

and the lowest-level economic agency to be granted this kind of autonomy.[3]

Brezhnev's successor, Yuri Andropov, tried to invigorate the machinery of Soviet foreign economic relations. On 26 May 1983, the first act was passed enabling the setting up of joint ventures with the CMEA countries on the territory of the USSR.[4] The procedure envisaged by this act was highly centralized and rigid, however, and it was not implemented in practice.

On 7 June 1984, under Chernenko, procedures were laid down for direct production and scientific and technological cooperation between ministries, departments and associations in the CMEA member countries, as well as in Yugoslavia. Industrial enterprises were granted the right to create their own funds for the development of international cooperation.[5] These funds could be used not only for the purchase of industrial goods and for the payment of extra bonuses to employees, but also for financing business trips to CMEA countries, for medical care and for holidays. This marked another small step in the delegation of authority to ministries, departments and the enterprises they ran.

Perestroika in foreign trade
During his rise to power Gorbachev had demonstrated his reformist inclinations by the backing that he gave to 'links' (self-accounting work teams) as the basic unit for the collective farms in his region, Stavropol, and to a similar experiment in the construction industry.[6] Describing the evolution of his thinking, Gorbachev wrote in *Perestroika* (1987):

> In my report of 22 April 1983, at a gala session dedicated to the 113th anniversary of Lenin's birth, I referred to Lenin's tenets on the need for taking into account the requirements of objective economic laws, on planning and cost accounting, and intelligent use of commodity-money relations and material and moral incentives. The audience enthusiastically supported this reference to Lenin's ideas. I felt, once again, that my reflections coincided with the sentiments of my fellow Party members ...

> Many of us realized even long before the April Plenary Meeting
> [1985] that everything pertaining to the economy, culture,
> democracy, foreign policy – all spheres – had to be
> reappraised.[7]

On 23 April 1985, in his report as General Secretary to a session of
the Party Central Committee, Gorbachev further developed his
ideas for economic reforms and for cooperation with the outside
world, leading to what he called 'the development of normal, equal
relations with capitalist countries'. He urged the cultivation of new
forms of external economic relations.

Gorbachev's report on the state of the Soviet economy delivered
in June 1985, did not, however, contain any ambitious proposals for
domestic economic reform. The key concept at this stage was
uskorenie (acceleration): the speeding-up of scientific and technological progress, and social and economic development. Here the
term *perestroika* (restructuring) did not yet denote the kind of
comprehensive policy of reform it later came to acquire. It was,
rather, associated with the rationalizing of management and planning. 'We should take a new approach to our external economic
strategy,' Gorbachev argued, but the focus was on goals rather than
methods: 'What is most important is to ensure profound structural
changes, and improve the pattern of our exports and imports.' He
complained that exports of Soviet machinery and equipment had
been growing only slowly in recent years. They competed poorly on
the market. Industrial enterprises had insufficient interest in produc-
ing export goods. 'We must not put up with this any longer,' he
declared. 'It is important actively to stimulate work collectives,
amalgamations and industries in general to increase the manufac-
ture of export products.'[8] There was no indication, however, of what
kind of stimulus was to be applied: whatever Gorbachev's own
preferences may have been, the political atmosphere was clearly not
yet appropriate for the announcement of radical innovations.

Institutional politics and academic debates

The exact nature of economic reform, internal and external, is

14

indeed still being hammered out in debate and political struggle. The main institutions involved in the discussions are for the most part either components of the party or state apparatus, or else academic bodies. The first group includes the State Foreign Economic Commission (Vneshekonomkomissiya or GVK), the Central Committee Commission on Economic Reform, Gosplan, the Ministry of Finance and the Ministry of Foreign Economic Relations (MFER). The second group includes the Institute of World Economy and International Relations (IMEMO), the Institute of the United States and Canada (ISKAN), the Institute of Europe, the Institute of the Economies of the World Socialist System (now the Institute of East Europe and International Relations), the Institute of Economics, the Academy of National Economy (ANKh) and the All-Union Institute for External Economic Contacts.

Government ministries and other bodies belonging to the first group tend to be more conservative and in general less keen to promote reform. Gosplan, for example, has a vested interest in preserving the old system of management, since the devolution of economic decision-making proposed by Gorbachev means stripping it of its enormous influence and power. One radical Soviet economist has described Gosplan as the 'centre of a monopolistic dictatorship exercised by the triumvirate of Gosplan, Gossnab and the Ministry of Finance, a dictatorship by means of departmental control of the economy and in the name of further monopolization'.[9] In February 1988, Gorbachev's initial appointee as head of Gosplan, Nikolai Talyzin, was dismissed just two years after being appointed, reportedly because Gosplan was hindering perestroika and resisting the decentralization of economic management.[10] He was replaced by his deputy, Yuri Maslyukov, who came to Gosplan in 1982 under Andropov.

There is, of course, a marked difference between, on the one hand, the traditional ministries and planning bodies and, on the other, the newly created bodies that have been specifically designed to promote economic reform, such as the GVK (the agency created for the purpose of overseeing reform in the sphere of foreign economic policy) and the Council of Ministers' Commission for Economic Reform, headed by Deputy Prime Minister Leonid Abalkin.

15

Although reformist by definition and design, those in the latter group have, of course, legislative and administrative responsibilities. Created in January 1987, the GVK has been headed since October 1989 by Stepan Sitaryan,†* a Gorbachev man who favours greater internationalization of the Soviet economy, and further decentralization of foreign economic activity.[11] The Deputy Chairman of the GVK, Ivan Ivanov, is an outspoken reformist and a frequent contributor – to both Soviet and foreign publications – of articles about the new foreign economic policy.[12] He stated in April 1989 that 'a course has been plotted to enable foreign trade to cease being primarily an instrument for solving the country's short-term problems and to become a long-term factor of its economic growth'.[13] This implied continued, wide-ranging decentralization of decision-making in the economy, a move to convertibility of the Soviet rouble, the establishment of a new tariff system, and close relations with the EC.

Academic institutions, free from the legislative and the executive burden, tend to be bolder in advocating reform or indeed in opposing it. They are joined – in increasingly unrestricted discussion about the necessary path to national salvation – by other sections of the Soviet intelligentsia, chiefly journalists and writers.

For some time there had been debate in the USSR on the broad issue of how much economic interdependence there could be between countries with different political systems.[14] By the 1980s positions were fairly clearly defined. There were those who opposed inter-system cooperation. Academician Gennady Sorokin,† for example, wrote in 1983 that the capitalist and socialist world-systems are economically 'incompatible and antagonistic'.[15] At the other end of the spectrum were those who favoured much greater cooperation with the outside world. These were the 'globalists', like Academician Andrei Sakharov, who emphasized the revolution in international relations brought about by the introduction of nuclear weapons. Sakharov wrote as early as 1968: 'The facts suggest that on any other course except ever-increasing coexistence and collabora-

---

* For information on some of the main figures relevant to this study, which are indicated in the text by a dagger (†), see the section 'Biographical Notes' at the back of the book.

tion between the two systems and the two super-powers, with a smoothing of contradictions and with mutual assistance, on any other course annihilation awaits mankind. There is no other way cut.'[16] In 1982 Fedor Burlatsky, currently editor of *Literaturnaya gazeta* and a member of the group of intellectuals close to Gorbachev, encapsulated the globalist economic platform when he wrote: 'No economy ... can develop without the closest economic ties with the economies of other countries, without participation in the international division of labour.'[17] Other writers took an intermediate position.[18]

Radicalization of the reform process in the years following 1985 was undoubtedly assisted by the fact that Gorbachev's informal 'kitchen cabinet'[19] included in 1987 four senior social scientists: Abel Aganbegyan,† Leonid Abalkin,† Oleg Bogomolov† and Aleksandr Anchishkin.† The ideas of another specialist, Tat'yana Zaslavskaya,† had influenced the leadership's thinking on reform, although she did not work closely with Gorbachev. All these people belonged to the Academic Committee of the Commission on Economic Reform.

Among academic bodies, ISKAN has served as an important institutional base for outspoken reformers. During a meeting of the US-USSR Trade and Economic Council held in Moscow in the spring of 1988, the director of ISKAN, Academician Georgi Arbatov,† argued eloquently in support of perestroika – 'a return to full-scale and unconditional realism'.[20] The economist Nikolai Shmelev,† a head of department at ISKAN and a People's Deputy, has become one of the most outspoken and radical proponents of reform. His writings have consistently tested the limits of glasnost on economic matters since its inception, and have left their mark on the evolution of Soviet economic thinking under Gorbachev.[21]

Economists like Oleg Bogomolov, Nikolai Shmelev and Abel Aganbegyan emphasize the need for financial incentives, and for reward proportional to the work done. Like the economist Yury Apenchenko, they declare that 'nobody – be he a foreman, director, minister or head of state – nobody should dare to say: "Aren't you having it too good?" If it is too good, take my place and earn it.'[22] They advocate decentralizing economic management, opening up

17

the domestic market to foreign goods, encouraging joint ventures with foreign firms, selling assets to foreigners, and setting up 'free economic zones'. As an argument for change, they point to the uncompetitiveness of Soviet manufactured exports and the consequent unbalanced structure of Soviet foreign trade.[23] This change cannot happen, they assert, without political reform. Criticizing the old bureaucracy, Nikolai Shmelev states, for example, that economic managers, especially the most senior ones, are possessed by a 'feudal psychology, the swaggering arrogance of caste, a belief in their own unsinkability, in their 'God-given' right to command, and in their immunity to the law and to criticism'.[24]

These ideas do not go unchallenged. A particular object of criticism are some of the proposals put forward by Shmelev – to lift restrictions on imports of foreign goods, so that they can provide competition with local products, to encourage the creation of firms with foreign capital, to create free economic zones, to make the rouble convertible in a short space of time. The conservative writer Mikhail Antonov recalled in 1988 how Lenin had been proud to read out the peasants' declaration at the Eighth All-Union Congress of the Soviets: 'We peasants are ready to starve, to freeze, to obey orders for another three years: just do not sell off Mother Russia to the concessions.' Now, by contrast, Antonov declared:

> People are already signing agreements on 'free economic zones'. This insults me personally, as a Russian and as a Soviet citizen, it affronts my patriotic feelings ... We are not an under-developed country, we are a great industrial power, and if we remove the interfering administrative and economic cobwebs from the people ..., then in a short time they will be able to flood the market with food-products and to create any super-modern technology without foreign mentors and culture-bearers.[25]

He also expressed total opposition to joint ventures with foreign countries: the USSR should not try to compete with the capitalist countries by using their methods but should stick to its own principles.[26]

Views of this kind are commonly published in a range of con-
servatively inclined Soviet journals, and they have deep cultural
roots.[27] The ideas they convey are reportedly widely shared in the
internal security forces and the armed forces, and are supported in
sections of the Communist Party apparatus, as the Andreeva affair
of 1988 demonstrated. They also figure in statements of some of the
new democratic parties. The election manifesto of the Bloc of
Russian Public Patriotic Movements, published in December 1989,
accused the Communist Party of the Soviet Union (CPSU) of
'yielding to the bloc of separatists and "left radicals" who are
prepared to dismember the USSR and sell off its national wealth to
Westerners'. The manifesto argued against decentralization of
foreign trade, and called for the abrogation of 'neo-colonial type'
joint-venture agreements without compensation.[28]

However, this trend has tended to remain in the background. In
the political sphere Gorbachev has steadily promoted supporters of
reform, except when, as in the case of Boris Yeltsin in 1987, they
overstepped the mark, and downgraded conservatives. In 1988, after
a frank public disagreement over economic reform with the leading
Politburo reformer, Aleksandr Yakovlev, the conservative Yegor
Ligachev was removed from his post as ideology chief, and lost his
position as Second Secretary of the Party. The shift in the seat of
power from the Politburo to the Presidential Council in 1990 was a
further blow to the conservatives. Gorbachev's new economic
adviser, Professor Nikolai Petrakov, appointed in late 1989, advo-
cated a faster pace of economic reform, including removal of state
ownership, de-monopolization of the economy, transition to a
market economy and the introduction of a parallel convertible
rouble. He argued that Gorbachev's team had a hundred days
within which to prove themselves.

In the first years after the introduction of perestroika, sweeping
reforms were carried out to streamline the ministries and departments, the strongholds of resistance to change. The number of
ministries was reduced, their staff was cut down and some privileges
of the top bureaucracy were removed.[29] On 17 January 1988 the
Ministry of Foreign Trade and the State Committee for Foreign
Economic Relations, which exercised the monopoly of foreign trade,

were abolished (with a loss of 5,000 jobs) and replaced by a new Ministry of Foreign Economic Relations, headed by Konstantin Katushev.[30]† Alongside these institutional changes, steady progress was being made in the second half of the 1980s in enacting a new legal framework for foreign economic relations.

Legislation

In the autumn of 1987, Gorbachev wrote that two and a half years after the policy of perestroika had been launched, he still considered it to be in its initial stage.[31] However, a short time later, in a speech delivered on 2 November 1987, marking the seventieth anniversary of the Bolshevik Revolution, he stated that work on the first stage of perestroika had been more or less completed, and that now the next stage was on its way. He defined the first stage as one of decision-making, and the second as one of implementation. According to Gorbachev the following two to three years (1988 to 1990/1) were to be the most critical ones. During that period the Soviet economy was to be switched from an excessively centralized command system of management to a 'democratic' one, relying principally on economic levers.[32] So little progress has been made so far, however, along the path to economic reform in general that it would probably be more accurate to describe the whole period up to 1990 as the first 'declaratory' period, and 1990–5 as a (potential) transitional period.

In the area of foreign economic ties, on the other hand, things have moved faster. Specific legislative decisions on reorganization were taken as early as August 1986. Two resolutions were issued on 19 August 1986, and three decrees on 13 January 1987, each dealing with different aspects of the new system of foreign economic relations. Later, at the end of 1987, another decision was adopted by the CPSU Central Committee and the Council of Ministers. The first five resolutions and decrees were to change the legal setting of Soviet external economic relations more profoundly than it had been altered since the period of NEP. The legislation can be summarized briefly as follows:

Resolution 1 (no. 991)
The monopoly of foreign trade as exercised by the Ministry of

Foreign Trade was broken by a resolution of 19 August 1986 (which came into effect on 1 January 1987). It allowed 21 ministries and departments, 66 enterprises, 7 inter-sectoral scientific and technical complexes, and 2 medical institutions to operate on the foreign market.[33] All in all, 97 ministries, departments and enterprises were granted the right to do business independently on foreign markets. Since the Councils of Ministers of the Union Republics were also permitted to establish financially autonomous foreign trade associations, the total number of actors was thus increased to over 100.[34] Most of the enterprises concerned were in the engineering sector.[35] State ministries, departments and the Union Republics would be permitted to keep up to 10% of the foreign currency funds of enterprises, but the remainder was not to be touched.

The same decree established the State Foreign Economic Commission, a standing body of the Council of Ministers of the USSR. Its job was to supervise the work of the Ministry of Foreign Trade, the State Committee for Foreign Economic Relations, the State Committee for Foreign Tourism, and other agencies working in the field of external economic relations.[36] The new State Foreign Economic Commission enjoyed far-reaching powers to plan, coordinate and control foreign economic activity in the USSR. It was able to grant permission to production associations, enterprises and organizations to conduct export and import operations independently. It had its own Research Institute for Foreign Economic Relations.[37]

This new legislation markedly reduced the prerogatives of the previously all-powerful Ministry of Foreign Trade. The latter did, however, retain control over trade in the most important commodities, such as fuel, raw materials, foodstuffs and a number of other items. The Ministry also participated in the signing and implementation of international treaties, exercised state control over the quality of export products, and issued permits allowing the export, import and transit of goods through the territory of the USSR. It also continued to control the network of Soviet trade representations at home and abroad.[38]

The foreign trade associations, until then virtually subordinates of the Ministry, were in future to conduct their business on cost-accounting and self-financing principles. The main goal of any foreign trade activity and criterion of its effectiveness would be its potential to earn foreign currency.

Resolution 2 (*no. 992*)

A second resolution, issued on 19 August 1986, was entitled 'On Measures to Improve the Management of Scientific and Technical Cooperation with Socialist Countries'.[39] It stated that whereas Gosplan would continue to fix targets for the overall volume of external economic transactions for ministries and departments, and identify targets for each CMEA country, it would not set targets for individual associations, enterprises and organizations. Firms would be allowed to use the currency they earned to purchase industrial goods, medical equipment and consumer goods from the CMEA countries, over and above centrally allocated quantities.

Decrees no. 6362-XI, no. 48 and no. 49

On 13 January 1987 two decrees were issued by the Council of Ministers. The first one (no. 48) concerned the establishment and operation of joint ventures with firms from CMEA member countries, and the second one (no. 49) covered similar dealings with firms from non-CMEA countries. In the first decree a distinction was drawn between joint ventures and international amalgamations: joint enterprises were to be set up to forward production and trade, whereas international amalgamations were to fulfil coordination and research functions.

The decree dealt also with legal aspects of the operation of joint ventures, amalgamations and organizations. It included a stipulation that 'their property shall not be requisitioned or confiscated by administrative decision' (section 10). The most important point in the document was that such organizations 'are independent in developing and approving their business operation programmes. State bodies of the USSR shall not fix any mandatory plans for them.' (section 18). This signified the long-sought-for break with Gosplan and the central ministries. Equipment, materials, and other property imported to the USSR by foreign partners in a joint venture as their contribution to the venture were, moreover, exempt from customs duties (section 28). The central authorities were still unwilling to give up their rights of control, and the procedure for setting up joint ventures was accordingly very cumbersome. However it was subsequently simplified (see below).

Decree no. 49 was in essence similar to no. 48. The stated purpose of the joint ventures in both decrees is exactly the same, and the chapters on taxation are identical. The second decree, however, does not mention 'international amalgamations and organizations', but only joint ventures. It states that the share of the Soviet side in the authorized fund of a joint venture shall be no less than 51%, that both the Director-General and the Chairman of the Board must be Soviet citizens, and that 'the personnel of joint ventures shall consist mainly of Soviet citizens'. Section 24 of the decree is significant in that it breaks up the state monopoly of foreign trade by granting the right of foreign trade to foreign participants in joint ventures.

Decision on Improvements (decree no. 1074)

By 17 September 1987, it had become clear that, however correct the basic principles underlying the earlier legislation in the area of foreign economic relations, its implementation and results were unsatisfactory. The Central Committee of the CPSU issued a decree 'On Additional Measures to Improve the Country's External Economic Activity in the New Conditions of Economic Management'.[40] The decree criticized the performance of economic agencies. Commenting on complaints expressed at the June 1987 Central Committee Plenum, it noted 'the stagnant phenomena still present in ... efforts to broaden ... external economic ties ..., insufficient initiative in developing exports and organizing new forms of cooperation'. It went on to state that the economic agencies 'make poor use of the rights granted them', and that 'they are slow in introducing economic methods of management and self-supporting systems'. It admitted the absence of appreciable changes in import policies, and declared that the process of taking decisions on foreign economic questions was excessively cumbersome.

The decision stated that all economic agencies should simplify existing procedures, develop the country's export base, radically improve the pattern of Soviet foreign trade, and (among other things) discontinue irrational imports. It stressed that the agencies should 'resolutely change to economic methods of management . . . actively establish joint ventures and lines of production as well as other effective forms of economic cooperation with all interested countries'. An important simplification of the procedure for establishing joint ventures was decided upon: USSR ministries and departments and the Councils of Ministers of the Union Republics were granted the right to take decisions on setting up joint ventures independently. Although a far cry from real self-management, this was, nevertheless, another step towards it. It meant further decentralization and delegation of the power of decision to the second tier of government bodies. The decision stated: 'It is considered necessary to conclude *intergovernmental* agreements with other socialist countries in the area of economic, scientific and technical cooperation *solely* on major inter-sectoral problems.' (Author's italics.)

The same was to apply to cooperation with capitalist and developing countries. This time, however, a wide range of types of cooperation was specified – setting up joint research and design organizations, engineering, sales and advertising firms, joint servicing and repair of exported machinery, sending abroad skilled specialists and workers, purchasing shares, bonds and other securities, their issue and flotation. The last of these was a far-reaching measure, which only a year earlier some Western specialists had considered highly unlikely. Even more revolutionary was the provision that associations, enterprises and organizations could invest currency abroad (with the consent of USSR ministries and departments).

As a result of the new legislation, by the end of 1987 about 900 economic agencies at different levels had direct foreign economic links.[41] Those ministries and departments that were granted the right of direct foreign economic activity accounted for 12% of total exports and 28% of total imports in 1987.[42]

The decision of 2 December 1988

The high point of Soviet foreign economic legislation to date was the decision of 2 December 1988, which introduced much more liberal conditions for joint ventures in the USSR, as well as certain

24

tax concessions. This decision is documented in greater detail in Chapter 4.

The decisions of 7 March 1989 (no. 203) and 11 December 1989 (no. 1104)

The Decision of 7 March 1989, 'On Measures of State Regulation of Foreign Economic Activity', which introduced licensing, was seen by Soviet reformers as a measure necessary for the control of trade in scarce goods. Yet it served to reassert greater state control over foreign economic transactions, and was the first regressive step in Soviet foreign economic legislation since 1985. It limited the export/import activities of joint ventures by making it impossible for them to trade except in their own products.

On 11 December 1989, because of problems in the general economic situation of the USSR, a further restrictive decision was adopted. This laid down that licences were required for the export and import of certain goods, whatever the type of foreign economic activity concerned (so that direct production and scientific and technical links, offshore and border trade or commodity exchange [barter] operations were all affected). The decision considerably tightened the March 1989 list of goods which require export licenses. Even worse was the stipulation that most of the licenses were to be issued by the MFER, which itself was involved in trade. This provision was in complete contradiction to the principle of decentralizing and demonopolizing the management of foreign economic links. As a consequence of criticism of the incompatibility of the MFER regulatory functions with this state of affairs, the decision was taken in May 1990 to set up a new agency independent of the MFER and accountable only to the Council of Ministers, which will be responsible for the issue of export licenses.

Cooperatives

The newly established cooperatives, which in practice are private businesses, were granted the right to participate in foreign economic activity in April 1989. The initial position of the Ministry of Finance reflected open hostility to this idea. It was summarized in August 1988 as follows: 'We have made many "concessions to capitalism" and if we allow our neo-bourgeois cooperative members to collaborate with their colleagues abroad, it will mark the end of socialism altogether.'[43] Indeed, to grant the cooperatives the right of direct involvement in foreign trade would, it appeared, remove another large brick from the edifice of the state monopoly of foreign trade, since it would allow private Soviet citizens to do business abroad. Out of the 2,548 cooperatives registered in Moscow by 5 July 1988, only one had been granted the right to engage in direct foreign economic activity.[44] In the course of 1989, however, cooperatives expanded rapidly. By 1 January 1990 there were 193,400 cooperatives, with 4,851,000 employees, registered in the USSR. Their total income from sales amounted to R40,366m, representing 4.4% of total GNP.[45] By April 1990, a year after the new rules came into effect, about 2,500 cooperatives had been registered as participants in foreign economic activity.[46]

Implementation of the legislation

It must be said that the main Soviet achievements so far have been legislative ones. Concrete results during the years since the legislation was passed have been modest. The major advance is the decentralization of foreign trade activity, in the context of a formal transition to self-accounting, self-management and self-financing. This represents a major transformation in Soviet foreign economic policy. In practice, however, considerable confusion prevails in the implementation of this policy. As the system is changing, neither the local participants in foreign economic activity nor the foreign companies feel that they are on firm ground. Soviet economic entities change their affiliation, laws continue to alter, corruption is widespread and the political context is unstable. No serious attempt has yet been made to take the domestic economic reform as a whole to its logical conclusion – a break with the past command system and the introduction of a market economy.

While the chief responsibility for the conduct of the Soviet economy rests with the Prime Minister, Nikolai Ryzhkov, a key part in top-level policy debates appears to be played by Leonid Abalkin, since 1989 Deputy Prime Minister and head of the USSR Council of

Ministers' State Commission on Economic Reform. Abalkin's outspoken and radical speech at a meeting on the reform on 19 November 1989 outlined eight broad measures to be implemented within a five-year period:

(1) denationalization of property;
(2) financial overhaul through a unified tax system, use of credit leverage through the banking system, and drastic stabilization of the money supply;
(3) an active structural policy to boost the consumer sector and increase export growth, and to cut waste of natural resources;
(4) the gradual creation of a market, with output produced in excess of state orders to be sold at free prices;
(5) gradual rapprochement between controlled state prices and free prices, and an adjustment to world market levels;
(6) the creation of a financial market, stock exchanges, and a state-controlled trade in securities;
(7) intensive development of foreign economic ties; and
(8) development of a currency market through auctions and regular trade to introduce partial convertibility of the rouble.[47]

Abalkin's ideas were in general accepted and reiterated in the CPSU Central Committee's platform for the twenty-eighth CPSU Congress, which was convened in July 1990. Nevertheless, by September 1990, although even more radical proposals have been put forward by leadership spokesmen – including those by the group headed by Academician Stanislav Shatalin and Professor Nikolai Petrakov – apart from official declarations there is still no evidence of a shift towards implementing the demanded changes.[48] Until such changes are brought about, the reform in foreign trade will continue to have limited practical significance. The chapters which follow will examine the progress that has been made so far in particular areas.

3

PATTERNS OF TRADE

The Soviet share of world trade has remained relatively small: it accounted for 3.9% of world exports and 4.3% of world imports in 1975; 4.6% and 4.3% respectively in 1985; and 3.8% and 3.7% in 1989 (according to January-September 1989 figures). By way of comparison, Japan accounted for 6.8% of world imports in 1975 and 7% in 1989, and its imports increased during the same period from 6.5% to 10%.[1] Despite the decade of detente, the share of East-West trade turnover in world trade turnover actually fell from 1.8% in 1970 to 1.6% in 1982.[2]

According to some Western scholars, the vast territory and rich natural resources of the Soviet Union make it comparatively independent of foreign trade. Vanous (1982) estimated that the volume of Soviet imports converted into dollars at the official exchange rate (which has hardly changed for years), after allowing for price divergences in intra-CMEA trade, accounted for only 4.1% of the dollar value of Soviet GNP estimated by the CIA.[3] Other economists, however, maintain that the importance of foreign trade for the Soviet economy is far greater than this would suggest.[4] This view was supported in 1988 by one Soviet writer, who noted that industrial goods accounted for more than 82% of Soviet imports. The share of machinery, equipment and means of transport had increased from 35.6% in 1970 to 40.7% in 1986, while the share of consumer goods had decreased in the same period from 18.3% to 13.4%. The textile industry, for example, imports 53.2% of its equipment, the chemical industry 49.9%, the food industry 46.8%; 31.3% of tramway carriages are imported, and 22.6% of steel pipes.[5] By the early 1980s Western equipment accounted for between 66% and 100% of Soviet output of polyethylene, polyester fibre and acrylic fibre, for 65% of the output of all complex and 40% of Soviet nitrogenous fertilizers.[6] The Soviet pharmaceutical industry meets only 45% of national requirements.[7] At the beginning of this century Russia was a major exporter of grain, while at present the Soviet Union is unable to feed its own population. In the 1970s the USSR imported 10%-15% of its grain requirements annually. In the 1980s the situation worsened, and it is not likely to change in the first half of the 1990s. At the June 1990 summit in Washington the Soviet Union signed a deal for the purchase of at least 10m tonnes of wheat, feed grains and soya beans annually (starting in 1991) from the US. That is an increase of 1m tonnes annually from the previous agreement, which took effect in 1983.[8] Because shortages in the shops have become politically sensitive, the import of food has begun to have strategic consequences for the Soviet regime.

On the other hand, minerals and fuel, extracted at great cost to the environment, account for about 80% of Soviet exports. The heavy dependence of Soviet industry on imports and the structural disequilibrium of Soviet foreign trade are rightly seen by Soviet reformers as major indicators of the inherent weakness of the economic system, reflecting in particular the poor quality of industrial products.

A strategy for change

According to senior Soviet economists, one of the major factors pushing in the direction of perestroika at home and in foreign trade is that 'since the beginning of the century, the relative demand for raw materials has been falling by approximately 1% annually, and that this process has now accelerated considerably. The prices of raw materials are now probably at the lowest level for the past 40 years, and the competition is acute.' Therefore, 'countries [like the USSR] which are producers of raw materials are naturally faced with major problems.'[9] The logical next step for the Soviet Union is to commence a drive, based on high technology, to transform its industrial capabilities. This would bring about a change in its export structure in favour of industrial goods, which would be more competitive and earn more hard currency. In his report at the June 1986 Plenary Meeting of the Central Committee of the CPSU, Gorbachev stated that, provided that the economic reforms were implemented, '80% to 95% of the total output of the basic goods will correspond to world standards by 1990, with the figure for newly developed products reaching practically 100%. It is planned to switch production entirely to top-quality articles between 1991 and 1993.'[10] At the beginning of the 1990s this goal can be seen to have been wildly over-ambitious.

Perestroika in foreign trade

From the very beginning of his term in office Gorbachev planned far-reaching expansion in the sphere of Soviet foreign economic relations, as he revealed in a speech on 23 April 1985:

> The Soviet Union is advocating fruitful and all-round economic, scientific and technological co-operation built on the principles of mutual benefit and excluding any sort of discrimination; it is prepared to continue to expand and develop trade relations, to develop new forms of economic relations on the mutual interest of the sides in the joint mastering of research, engineering and technological innovations, the design and construction of enterprises and in the exploitation of raw material resources ... The approach to mutually advantageous economic relations and foreign trade must be extensive, large scale and projected into the future.[11]

At the same time, the recent, and not so recent, experience of Western economic sanctions has left its mark on policy. At the June

1985 meeting Gorbachev also stated that 'social and economic development must be accelerated because it is necessary for our economy to become totally independent of the capitalist countries, especially in strategic areas'.[12] The same idea, in more blunt terms, was put forward in the new edition of the Party Programme of 1 March 1986. It stated:

> While considering equal and mutually beneficial economic cooperation between socialist and capitalist states to be natural and useful, the CPSU at the same time believes that development of socialist integration should enhance the technical and economic invulnerability of the community with regard to hostile actions by imperialism and to the influence of economic crises and other negative phenomena that are intrinsic to capitalism.[13]

At this stage, then, Gorbachev was calling for an international division of labour, primarily within the framework of the socialist countries.

During his visit to Paris in October of the same year Gorbachev once more stressed that the Soviet Union gave 'priority to the demands of scientific and technological progress both at home and in [its] foreign economic relations'.[14] And, indeed, the scientific and technological areas received the largest share of official attention. There soon followed new legislation in the area of external economic relations, which encouraged foreign economic activity. Nevertheless, Soviet foreign trade turnover decreased from R142.1bn in 1985, to R128bn in 1987 (a decline of 10%). It recovered to R140.9bn in 1989 (see Appendix 6: A.1), but the annual increase in Soviet foreign trade in 1989 of 6.6% still lagged behind the 8% increase in world trade the same year. This gap in the rates of growth may, of course, diminish if Soviet foreign trade continues to expand at the present rate and the growth in world trade slows to 6% in 1990. The challenge for the USSR of maintaining its present share of world trade will, however, increase with the expected growth in world trade of 7.5% in 1991 and 1992.[15]

The USSR is the largest crude oil producer in the world. With 11.6m barrels per day, it accounted for 19.8% of the world production in 1989 (a drop from 21.6% in 1987).[16] It consumes domestically about 70% of the extracted oil, and the remainder is exported. Soviet production of natural gas liquids accounts for 10.6% of the world total. It produces 2,104bn cubic metres per day, of which it consumes 89.1% (1988 figures), while the rest is exported.[17]

The Soviet Union's dependence on hard-currency earnings that are derived from the sale of oil and gas has increased dramatically in the last two decades. Annual Soviet hard-currency earnings from the export of oil and oil products increased from $556m in 1972 to $14,085m in 1983. During the same period the share of oil and oil products in hard-currency earnings increased from 19.9% to 64.2%, while the total hard-currency earnings from energy exports rose from 28.9% ($809m) to 79.1% ($17,386m).[18] The Soviet Union had benefited from windfall profits, with the rise of the price of oil in the 1970s and early 1980s. However, the increased reliance on the sale of energy raw materials proved to be short-sighted. The spot price per barrel, which had averaged $27 in 1985, declined to well below $10 in July 1986, before increasing to $14-$15 after the OPEC (Organization of Petroleum Exporting Countries) agreement in August 1986 to curb production and stabilize prices. During 1987 it fluctuated in the area of $16 to $19 per barrel, declining to an average of $14.5 in 1988, but increasing to $17.4 in 1989.[19] The fall in the price of oil was the main factor contributing to the decreasing Soviet foreign-trade earnings. According to the Soviet Finance Minister, Boris Gostev, the USSR lost a total of R40bn in the period 1985–8 because of the sharp drop in world oil prices.[20]

The Soviet Union experienced a decline in its terms of trade (ratio of export prices to import prices) in the twelfth Five-Year Plan, not only from the oil price cut but also because of the weakening of the US dollar against European currencies: it sells oil in dollar terms, but most of its equipment purchases are in European currencies.[21] Indeed, some 70% of Soviet convertible currency purchases are made in currencies other than the dollar.[22] Most of the decline in 1987 (as compared with 1985) was registered in trade with the industrial capitalist countries, which dropped by 25.9% (see Tables 3.1 to 3.3* and Appendix 6: A.2). Although showing a physical increase of about 9.3% in 1986 and a further 2.1% in 1987, exports in 1986 yielded R4.4bn less in earnings than in 1985, further decreasing by 0.1bn roubles in 1987. As *Izvestiya* pointed out, 'this signifies ... that the goods we export are being valued more and more cheaply on the world market.'[23]

In the postwar years Soviet foreign trade showed a steady increase (in nominal value) from R1.3bn in 1946 to R141.6bn in 1985 (see Appendix 6: A.1).[24] Between 1960 and 1985 it increased 4.72 times in real terms.[25] The share of CMEA countries in total Soviet trade turnover amounted to 56% in 1955, gradually decreased to 48.6% in 1980, then climbed again to 61.8% in 1987, but (with the mounting difficulties in intra-CMEA trade) decreased to 55.8% in 1989. The share of industrialized Western countries was 15.5% in 1955, increased unsteadily to 33.6% in 1980, and then dropped to 21.8% in 1987, but recovered to 26.2% in 1989.[26] Thus, the diminishing share of the Western countries was replaced during the mid-1980s by trade with the CMEA member countries. This trend was reversed by the close of the decade.

The share of developing countries in Soviet foreign trade was 4.7% in 1955, and this rose to around 13% on average in the 1980s; in 1989 it stood at 12.1%.

In the period 1985–9 trade with seven Western countries accounted for nearly three-quarters of total Soviet foreign trade turnover with developed Western countries (72.2% in 1989). The seven were West Germany, Finland, Italy, Japan, the USA, Britain and France (see Table 3.5), although their respective place in the table has changed during that period (for example, France slid from fourth place in 1985 to seventh in 1989, while Italy went up from fourth to third place). The foreign-trade figures show that an attempt was made to balance out East-West trade. During the period 1985–9, both exports to and imports from the developed Western countries decreased from their level in 1985 of R18.6bn and R19.3bn respect-

* For tables in this chapter, see Appendix 4.

ively to R14.2bn and R13.9bn in 1987, but recovered to R16.4bn and R20.5bn in 1989 (see Tables 3.6 and 3.7).

The most notable increase in imports in 1989 as compared with 1985 was registered in respect of West Germany (from R3.1bn to R4.1bn) and Britain (from R0.7bn to R1bn). Imports, however, decreased dramatically in the case of Canada by 56.6% (from R0.9bn in 1985 to R0.4bn in 1989). The most notable decrease in exports was registered in respect of West Germany (from R4bn to R2.5bn) and France (from R2.2bn to R1.4bn). However, in spite of the fluctuating export/import trend with the other countries, exports to Britain have consistently increased from R1.2bn to R2.2bn (an increase by 81.4% over the same five-year period).

In recognition of the growing importance of the Far Eastern markets, the Soviet Union has established economic relations with South Korea. Whereas before perestroika trade was non-existent, it shot up to $200m in 1987, and leapt further to $600m by 1989. It is expected to top $1bn in 1990, and, according to South Korean estimates, may reach $10bn by the mid 1990s.[27] Trade relations with the other NICs are also being actively developed. Economic relations with Israel have been re-established and are also expanding. Regrettably, in spite of glasnost, the data on trade with South Korea and Israel have not been included in the annual Soviet publications for 1988 and 1989.

The imbalance of Soviet trade with the industrial West is shown in Table 3.8. During the period 1985–9 the USSR accumulated a negative trade balance of R8.9bn with the Western countries. In some cases this is particularly high: with the US: -R7.3bn, Japan: -R7.8bn, Canada: -R2.8bn, Finland: -R2.5bn and Australia: -R2.3bn. On the other hand a positive balance was registered in the trade with Great Britain: R4.8bn, Netherlands: R2.4bn, Italy: R2bn, France: R1.9bn (see Table 3.8).

Table 3.8 demonstrates that a serious attempt was made in 1987 to reduce the trade imbalance with the Western countries. In fact, the negative balance of the years 1985–6 was succeeded by a small surplus in that year. This was at a time when the most important Soviet export asset – oil – hardly changed its price, although other commodity prices had increased by about 19% in 1987. The most

34

significant reduction in the trade imbalance was registered in trade with the United States and Japan. To encourage production of machinery and machine-related products for export in exchange for freely convertible currency, starting from 1986, enterprises were to receive additional subsidies of 20% on their wholesale prices.[28] In spite of the effort to improve the Soviet hard-currency trade balance, the increased imports from the West in 1988 and 1989 led to a considerable drain on hard-currency reserves, which brought about difficulties in settling payments in the first half of 1990 of more than $2bn.[29]

Trade with the CMEA
With the political reorientation of Soviet foreign policy, and the change in the domestic economic priorities, intra-CMEA trade is also being affected by perestroika. Soviet trade turnover with the CMEA countries remained at almost the same level throughout 1985–9, but the export/import values have changed: Soviet exports have decreased from R40.2bn in 1985 to R38.0bn in 1989 (a decrease of 5.6%), while imports increased from R37.9bn to R40.6bn (an increase of 7.1%) during the same period (see Tables 3.9 and 3.10). Thus in 1985–7 the USSR maintained a positive trade balance with the CMEA countries, but in 1988 and 1989 the balance was negative. This trend is explained by the fall in prices of energy raw materials. As Tables 3.11 and 3.12 illustrate, most of Soviet trade within the CMEA is conducted with East Germany, Bulgaria, Poland and Czechoslovakia (67.9% of total trade with CMEA countries in 1989), although their relative standing has also changed during the period 1985–9.

Soviet reformers have recognized that there is no need heavily to subsidize the East European countries or to tie them down through forced economic integration. Who has subsidized whom is a matter for debate. Soviet aid to its allies is expressed not just in transfer of money or equipment but also by subsidizing Soviet purchases, sometimes to absurd extents. Thus, for example, in 1989 the USSR purchased from Cuba 4.3m tonnes of sugar, which accounted for one-third of total Soviet consumption of sugar. The USSR paid 7 to

9 times more for the Cuban sugar than the world price, thereby providing hidden aid to Cuba to the tune of over R2bn ($3.2bn). The issue concerning Soviet aid to Cuba was taken up by President George Bush in June 1990 as a matter that has to be settled before providing large-scale aid to the USSR.[30] Another example of Soviet aid to its allies is the project to build a chicken factory in Mongolia, the planned break-even point for which is 200 years ahead.[31]

At different times, however, different parties have gained or lost. The future of the CMEA is uncertain, but one thing is clear – the organization will never be the same again. From 1991 trade within the CMEA (if that organization survives at all) is to be conducted using world prices and hard-currency settlements. This will, no doubt, influence the pattern of trade between the USSR and the other CMEA member countries, especially in machinery and equipment. The socialist countries serve as an important market for Soviet machinery and equipment. In 1989, out of total machinery and equipment exports of R10.9bn, the socialist countries accounted for R8.5bn (77.9%). At the same time the socialist countries are the chief suppliers of these commodities to the Soviet Union: out of total Soviet imports of R28.5bn the socialist countries accounted for R20.7bn (72.6%), representing a slight increase on 1988 figures from 20.4bn in nominal value, but a relative decrease on the total share of machinery imports of 76.7%. With the transfer to hard-currency settlements it is thought that the trade in machinery and equipment among the socialist countries will decline in the near future, to be replaced by trade with the Western countries.[32]

Eastern Europe is also a major customer for Soviet energy exports. Out of total exports of 103,000m cubic metres of natural gas in 1989, which accounted for 12% of the country's hard-currency earnings, 50,000m cubic metres went to Bulgaria, Hungary, the GDR, Poland, Romania, Czechoslovakia and Yugoslavia.[33]

Difficulties in Soviet trade with the CMEA countries have been well illustrated in an account of problems in Soviet-Hungarian trade published in *Izvestiya* in 1990.[34] Some 70% of Soviet exports to Hungary are raw materials (mainly oil). The prices of raw materials have dropped in recent years. In addition there were shortfalls in Soviet deliveries of many goods in 1989 – namely 267,000 cubic metres of timber, 100,000 tonnes of coal and 46,000 tonnes of petrol. This produced a deficit in trade with Hungary in 1989 – a debt of 782m transferable roubles (TR) on the Soviet side. At the same time Hungary, which has an external debt of about $21bn, has argued that it is in no position to lend the USSR about R1bn a year. Hungary's receipt of IMF credits is also conditional on its conducting a balanced trade in roubles. As a result, in January 1990 the Hungarian Council of Ministers introduced the licensing of rouble-denominated exports, which led to widespread stoppages in production of goods for the Soviet market.

On the other hand, machinery and equipment account for about 50% of Hungary's exports to the USSR, and CMEA prices for these are on average 50% higher than world prices. In addition, the Soviet side argues that 75% of Soviet exports to Hungary could be sold on the world market for hard currency, while just 25% of Hungarian exports to the USSR could be so sold. Hungary also owes the USSR R360m in long-term credits. Eventually an agreement was reached to calculate the outstanding debt balance in dollars at a rate of R1 to $0.92. Thus the Soviet debt for 1989 was agreed at $720m. As a result, Soviet-Hungarian trade has effectively been put on a hard-currency basis earlier than planned.

Finally, although some change will occur in Soviet trade with the CMEA member countries in the future, their high dependence on Soviet energy will not disappear. If there is a shift in Soviet imports of consumer goods and equipment from CMEA to other countries, this will lead to a trade imbalance between the USSR and CMEA countries. The latter will have to increase their borrowings of hard currency from the West. At the same time the USSR will also be squeezed for hard currency, and where possible will prefer barter deals with the East European states according to established patterns.

There has, then, been no significant change in the structure of Soviet foreign trade since 1985. This will clearly require a much longer time. Structural changes depend on the quality and sophistication of goods, as well as on successful marketing. What is beyond doubt is the high priority that improving the pattern of trade enjoys in Soviet policy. If economic reform continues to develop in the direction of decentralization and free-market relations, and political developments lead to most-favoured-nation (MFN) status in the developed Western countries, a slight shift in foreign trade structure might, however, become noticeable by the mid-1990s. This could be encouraged by the growth of joint ventures, which by that time will be starting to deliver their goods onto the market. Progress in this area of policy will be discussed in the next chapter.

4

JOINT VENTURES

The Soviet policy of joint ventures (JVs) must be seen in the context of a much wider process of growing international economic interdependence. Thus, in the period between 1983 and 1988, global foreign direct investment (FDI) increased by over 20% per annum in real terms, while world trade volumes grew annually by only 5%.[1] In the countries of the Group of Five (G-5), roughly four million industrial workers are employed by foreign-owned firms, representing 8% of total manufacturing employment. Between 1984 and 1988, total FDI in America almost doubled, from $165bn to $329bn. In the chemical industry, for example, foreign companies' share of the American workforce increased from 20% in 1980 to about 45% in 1989; in building materials, from almost nothing to 50%.[2]

By July 1990, Soviet firms had signed some 1,830 JV agreements with Western and East European firms from over 60 countries. The total foundation capital exceeded $5,000m, with total production volume in 1990 of about $1,000m, divided 9:1 between the domestic market and exports.[3] JVs accounted for R546.5m (0.4%) of Soviet foreign trade in 1989. Exports amounted to R126.5m (0.2%) and imports to R420m (0.6%).[4] It remains to be seen, however, whether the new policy has yielded much in terms of improving the range and quality of Soviet products or the efficiency of production.

Soviet objectives

The Soviet Union needs active Western cooperation in its efforts to restructure and modernize its economy. JVs are envisaged as playing a central part in attracting such cooperation. One condition specified at an early stage by Soviet spokesmen was that JV products should be absolutely new and should have both a Soviet and a world market.[5] The 'absolutely new product' requirement reflected the initially limited goals of the JV policy, and, as we shall see, this narrow conception was subsequently abandoned. For the Soviet Union, JVs provide a convenient way to transfer Western 'know-how' and advanced technology to Soviet industry; to introduce advanced Western economic management methods; to produce goods and services that cannot adequately be provided by domestic industry; and to carry out import substitution. The stated objectives of the policy also include a much-needed increase in Soviet exports to augment hard-currency revenues; a change in the composition of Soviet exports (by increasing the number of finished goods exported rather than raw materials); increased competitiveness for Soviet goods on foreign markets; and better access to foreign markets (through services, business connections and the marketing branches of the JVs' foreign partners).

With the increasing number of Soviet cooperative (i.e., private) enterprises participating in JV activity, a distinction is emerging between the objectives of these private bodies and those of state enterprises participating in JVs. As distinct from long-term interests of the kind set out above, the private sector is concerned mainly with short-term financial gain. Although private objectives do not necessarily contradict state objectives, they do not coincide. This leads to the proliferation of trade transactions and of JVs specializing in the provision of services rather than in industrial production.

Primarily intended to improve the performance of the domestic economy, the emergence of the JV policy also signals that the USSR is willing to take a more active role in the world economy. The involvement of a large number of Western businessmen in JVs (as well as in trade) will inevitably exert some influence on foreign governments to be more accommodating towards the USSR, for example by reducing tariffs and by modifying technology embargoes.

Western objectives
The main objectives of Western partners in Soviet JVs are to gain access to the local market, and to expand trade in and with the USSR. Attractions for Western businesses include a large and unsatisfied consumer market in the USSR; a high level of basic scientific education there; large deposits of raw materials, which may be processed by a JV and exported through a JV to other countries; the opportunities to construct facilities, such as hotels and international convention centres, which can earn hard currency; the fact that land need not be purchased;* and geographical closeness to West European and East Asian markets. More broadly, cooperation through JVs may also help to reduce cultural and political misunderstandings between East and West, as well as, by force of example, influencing the conduct of Soviet domestic economic (and social) policy. Direct contact between Western businessmen and local people also helps to dispel the distorted images of the West broadcast by old-style Soviet propaganda.

The background
Several joint-stock companies with foreign firms were already in existence in the 1960s, but these were located abroad, and the participants or shareholders on the Soviet side were exclusively state agencies. The companies were important for Soviet foreign trade in providing a foreign base and foreign representation in external markets, but in general their turnover was not large. By the end of 1981, the Soviet Union participated in 111 economic agencies in the OECD countries, the majority of which (104) were active in various types of services (import, marketing, retailing, finance, transport);

---

* There is no land or property market in the USSR. This, however, may also be viewed as a disadvantage: if a company may not own land, it has no asset to rely on.

only two were engaged in assembly and manufacturing, and five in extraction and processing of raw materials. The share of Soviet ownership was usually more than 50%, with average invested capital of about $1.4m, which represents a very low overall level of Soviet participation in Western industry.[6]

Proposals for the introduction of JVs had been put forward in the USSR since the early 1980s, but were implemented only in 1987.[7] The beginnings of a move away from centralized bureaucratic management in the domestic economy and the introduction of JVs with foreign firms on Soviet territory represent an important opening-up of the Soviet economy and a major departure from past policy. The introduction of JVs loosened the state's grip on foreign trade (already being weakened by the dismantling of the system whereby most of the USSR's foreign trade had been conducted through one agency – the Ministry of Foreign Trade). The setting-up of cooperatives with rights to do business in foreign markets weakened control even further. Furthermore, now that state enterprises may issue shares to their employees, the latter can be considered to be participants in foreign economic relations, and especially so through JVs.

Legislative evolution

Open-mindedness and readiness to revise unsuccessful legislation has become the most characteristic feature of recent Soviet policy on JVs. This open approach gives hope for the continuation and positive evolution of the policy.

The JV legislation was introduced by three decrees in mid-1986 and the beginning of 1987 (discussed in Chapter 2). To date, there have been three amendments: in September 1987, December 1988 and March 1989. Of these amendments, the first two introduced easier terms of operation for the JVs (see Table 4.1*), indicating a new flexibility on the part of the Soviet leadership. The third decree (March 1989) contained some regressive features: it limited JVs' exports to their own products, and imports to their own needs, thereby excluding the JVs from a wider participation in Soviet

* For tables in this chapter, see Appendix 5.

foreign trade, and, more importantly, preventing them from using rouble incomes to purchase Soviet goods that could be sold for hard currency abroad.

The primary aim of Soviet economic cooperation during the twelfth Five-Year Plan (1986–90) was declared to be the strengthening of cooperation and increased economic integration with the CMEA member countries. The USSR signed international agreements on the establishment and operation of JVs with Poland (15 October 1986), Czechoslovakia, Bulgaria and Hungary (4 November 1986), and the GDR (17 December 1986),[8] but not with Romania. Agreements with Cuba and Mongolia antedate these.

However, progress in the area of intra-CMEA cooperation has been modest, particularly in the area of JVs. Of a total of 384 JVs registered by mid-April 1989, only 57 (14.8%) were with socialist countries.[9] By October of the same year their share had dropped to 9.1% (86 JVs out of a total of 947).[10]

A decree of 13 January 1987 authorized the creation of JVs with foreign firms on the territory of the USSR.[11] In general, Western joint enterprises are neither subject to Soviet planning instruction nor guaranteed purchases and sales. This decree was more significant than previous legislation on links with foreign firms, since it introduced a private (foreign) element into domestic economic activity. On the Soviet side, it was a state agency or enterprise representing the other partner in a JV. These JVs were to contain several built-in constraints (for instance, a minority foreign share, a Soviet general director, calculation of foreign investment in roubles and a relatively short tax exemption of two years).

By mid-1987 it seemed to have become clear to the Soviet authorities that because of restrictive Soviet JV legislation on the one hand, and Western trade restrictions on trade with the East European countries coupled with lack of confidence by Western businessmen in Soviet proposals on the other, the initial drive for the swift creation of joint enterprises was not meeting with success. Thereafter, JVs were allowed to be concluded with greater ease and in more sectors of the national economy. There is a clear correlation between the loosening of legal restrictions and the number of JVs registered: the figure increased from 23 in 1987 to 191 by the end of

1988, and to over 1,600 by June 1990. By that time more than 60 countries were participating in Soviet JVs, the majority being concluded with companies from West Germany, Finland, Britain and the USA.

The first agreements with Western governments on mutual protection of capital investments were signed at the beginning of 1989 with Finland, Belgium and Britain; other Western countries were starting to negotiate similar agreements.

The average initial capital of a JV in the second half of 1989 was R2.6m, down from R4.2m in the period 1987–8. It should be noted that in some cases the capital took the form of the share of machinery which one of the participants contributed to the venture: in some cases it was foreign and in others it was Soviet. The total ownership capital for 947 JVs registered by 10 October 1989 was R2,520m, as compared with R811.5m for 191 JVs at the close of 1988. The foreign share was R1,023m or 42%, an increase from R306.2m or 37.7% over the same period.[12] This is still rather small when compared with the face value of foreign investment in China for 1988 alone, which totalled $5.2bn (R3.15bn) for 5,890 contracts.[13] FDI inflows into France in 1987, for example, amounted to a total of some $4.3bn (FFr26.3bn).[14] Soviet internal investment in technical renovation and reconstruction in 1987 totalled R43.5bn.[15]

Of the 191 joint ventures, only 23 have foundation capital of more than R10m, but these account for 60% of the total capital invested (and may be considered large ventures); whereas 85 medium-sized ventures have capital ranging between R1m and R10m, accounting for 36.4% of the total capital; and 83 small ventures have capital of less than R1m, and account for only 3.6% of the total capital. A small amount of foundation capital, of course, does not indicate that the JV's turnover will be small. Some are based on know-how, development of computer programs, trade or services, which may not require a large amount of foundation capital. In any case, additional capital may be borrowed from the bank at a later stage.

The degree of risk involved in JV activity in the USSR is still not clear, and most Western companies are reluctant to make large investments. There is still lack of confidence in the USSR's political stability, and in the impartiality of the judiciary. As a result of the

British-Soviet row in May 1989 over spying charges against Soviet personnel in London, the Soviet authorities threatened to limit the numbers of British businessmen in Moscow. There was an uproar among the Western, and no doubt among the Soviet, business community. It was only at the last moment that foreign and Soviet staff of JVs were reprieved.[16]

Among the most frequently discussed and most worrying issues for Western businessmen involved in JVs are taxation, currency problems (regarding repatriation), participation share, labour questions, quality control, supplies, areas/zones of economic activity and the evolving nature of the policy on JVs. These issues will now be discussed individually.

Taxes

The maximum tax rate for JVs is 44%, payable in roubles (30% on the net profit and another 20% on profits repatriated abroad).[17] However, this tax is open to negotiation in every case: the USSR Ministry of Finance has the right to reduce the tax on profit and to release particular tax payers from payment of the tax. This vague legislation has both positive and negative consequences. The goodwill of the Ministry of Finance, which is responsible for collecting these taxes, depends on the Soviet partner's ability to convince ministry officials of the importance of the particular JV. It opens the way to flexibility, but it introduces uncertainty into the economic calculations of the partners, as well as creating conditions for arbitrary decision-making, corruption and intrigue.

The existing two-year tax exemption rule was altered by decree no. 1074 of 17 September 1987, which stated that JVs shall, as a rule, be exempt from profit tax during the first two years from the moment the declared profit is received, and not from the date of their registration. This was a considerable improvement in incentives, although the 20% tax level on repatriation of the profits was not amended.[18] A third decree, published in December 1988, changed the taxation rules for JVs set up in the Soviet Far East: the tax exemption was extended to three years, and the tax on profits was reduced from 30% to 10%. These changes reflected the perception that some initial impetus needed to be given to establishing a special economic zone in the region, to assist economic development by drawing on the potential of Japan, South Korea, Singapore, Taiwan, the US, China and other Pacific states.

Currency

One of the chief obstacles to the creation of JVs is the non-convertibility of the rouble. Soviet legislators had initially hoped that JVs would mainly produce goods for export in order to obtain foreign currency, whereas Western businessmen, lacking confidence in the ability of Soviet goods to compete on foreign markets, prefer to cater for the Soviet market. The inability to realize roubles often results in payment in kind. Thus, for example, Western electronics companies have admitted that they take out profits in the form of animal skins, which they sell on to the Italian shoe industry.[19]

Some of the JVs may earn hard currency by selling goods and services to foreign tourists, diplomats and companies in the USSR (examples being car-hire services, duty-free shops and restaurants). When the purchase for roubles of Soviet export goods and their resale abroad, allowed by the December 1988 decree, was prohibited in March 1989, companies found it practically impossible to use their rouble profits outside the USSR. On the other hand, sub-contractors and suppliers to a JV are allowed to charge part of the payment due to them in hard currency. Although the prospect of earning hard currency motivates local enterprises to supply to JVs, this regulation (introduced in December 1988) creates a problem for the JVs, which need hard currency for their own imports and to repatriate profits. This creates an additional burden and obstacle to profitability.

It should be noted that the foreign partner's share may be assessed in hard currency, and the Soviet partner's in roubles. Joint ventures may maintain dual currency accounts, and this is considered by Western partners to be of major importance (particularly for JVs that have a service orientation extending beyond the country). Hard-currency income of the foreign partner may also be repatriated abroad. It is not clear how the foreign partner's share in profits will be calculated if the JV works solely for the domestic (Soviet) market, and receives roubles.

The official rouble exchange rate fluctuated for years between US $1.2 and US $1.6, in contrast to the black market rate of between 10 and 15 cents per rouble.[20] The December 1988 decree envisaged that the first step towards rouble convertibility would be taken on 1 January 1990, by a 100% increase in the exchange rate of hard currency against the rouble. This, however, has not been carried out. Instead, a new non-commercial, tourist exchange rate was introduced in November 1989 ($1 = R6.25). In January 1991 a new exchange rate is to be set for settlements relating to foreign economic transactions. However, full convertibility is not expected to be achieved until the end of the 1990s.

A more immediate and practical step towards establishing the real value of the rouble was taken in the course of 1989 through the holding of foreign currency auctions. The auctions were restricted initially to Soviet enterprises; JVs, foreign companies and cooperatives were to be allowed to participate only at a later stage. Contrary to the official Soviet view of their benefits, currency auctions in a still highly controlled and unreformed economy may contribute to excess demand for hard currency. As expected, during the first auction in November 1989, demand for hard currency exceeded supply: 210 offers were made to buy foreign currency, but only 31 to sell. Only R8.5m exchanged hands, at an average rate of R15.2 to $1.[21] The rouble's exchange rate dropped further, to R27.11 to $1 at the third auction held in May 1990 (see Table 4.2).

With growing internal instability, it is likely that the free-market rouble exchange rate will continue to deteriorate unless some drastic measures are taken to stabilize the currency. Rouble convertibility may have to be introduced well before the end of the century because the present inconvertibility will continue to hamper economic reform.

Participation share

Initially, majority Soviet equity in JVs was seen as a *sine qua non* by the Soviet leadership.[22] Until the end of 1988, in all cases except three JVs with East European countries, the Soviet share in a JV was between 51% and 98.5%. After widespread criticism both at home and abroad, however, the December 1988 decree permitted the foreign partner to hold a majority share in a JV. Subsequently, agreements were signed in which the Soviet partner holds as little as 20% of the equity (and in principle it may be even less than that).

A significant change in the legislation is the provision allowing the foreign partner to sell his share to any third party, with the consent of the two sides.

Labour

Another contentious issue that was settled by the December 1988 decree relates to the labour question. Issues concerning the hiring and firing of staff, and the forms and size of remuneration and material incentives in Soviet roubles, can now be decided by the JV itself.[23]

Most of the employees of a JV with a Western country are to be Soviet citizens (decree no. 49, 13 January 1987). There is a high demand for jobs in JVs: salaries are two to three times higher than the national average, and there are opportunities for foreign travel and access to foreign consumer goods. Indeed, JVs often send the managerial personnel abroad for advanced training (as is the practice of McDonalds of Canada and Salamander of West Germany). Yet shortages of trained local staff are a major obstacle for JVs. The cost of maintaining Western personnel in the USSR is very high. It is estimated at some $400,000 a year for a one-worker office (including at least four home visits, the renovation of an apartment, and the importing of basic but hard-to-find items for the employees' families).[24] JVs also have difficulty finding Western staff to work in remote areas of the country, where the communication network is very poor, housing conditions are substandard, and consumer goods and food have to be specially supplied.[25]

Initially, the foreign personnel of JVs had to pay in hard currency for housing and other services provided for them in the Soviet Union. Now, however, these may be paid for in Soviet roubles. As the demand for housing grows, it is becoming increasingly difficult to find adequate accommodation in central locations for foreign personnel as well as for offices.

Quality

Raising the quality of production presents a major challenge to any foreign firm wishing to operate in the USSR. A Soviet economist wrote in June 1987 that 'according to the most "patriotic" evaluation, only 17%-18% of our manufacturing industry conforms to world standards, whilst according to the most cautious and pessimistic ones the figure is 7%-8%'.[26] The officially stated goal of 80%-90% of Soviet industry reaching world standards in the course of the twelfth Five-Year Plan has proved to be unrealistic. Reject rates of 30%-40% are common, and often 20%-30% of electronic and other equipment fails soon after introduction into service.[27] According to data published by the USSR State Committee for Statistics, in the period January-May 1989 consumer complaints were registered as follows: tape recorders, 23%; coloured TVs, 20.9%; semi-automatic washing machines, 9.2%; and radio receivers, 7.6%.[28] Some JVs have attempted to overcome quality problems by establishing a number of joint companies that can supply each other with the necessary components.[29] This arrangement seems, so far, to be the only feasible alternative to having to import most of the sub-components in exchange for hard currency. The Soviet partner is often unwilling to purchase the necessary parts from abroad for two main reasons: the lack of hard currency, and the pressure to support local industry.

Supplies

JVs are not included in the state planning system, which creates supply difficulties for the Soviet partner. And a wholesale-trade market is still non-existent.[30] Some progress in this respect has been made: in May 1990, a commodity exchange was set up in Donetsk, and, at the beginning of June 1990, another was set up in Moscow.[31] These, however, are still in their preliminary stages. Thus, for example, when the Soviet-Canadian Moscow-based McDonalds JV needed ketchup for its hamburgers, it had the choice of importing it from abroad or building a special processing facility for the purpose. In fact, McDonalds has built a food-processing and packaging plant, as well as setting up its own local delivery system, at a cost of $45m. All this in addition to its Moscow restaurant, which cost $5m.

Special Economic Zones

At present some 50% of JVs have Moscow addresses, while others are located mainly in the European part of the USSR, with Leningrad and Tallinn at the top of the list. This is likely to be modified by the creation of Special Economic Zones (SEZs), which are intended as 'bridges' between the domestic economy and the outside world, and are an important tool in the rehabilitation of the Soviet economy. It is planned to set up SEZs in areas conveniently adjacent to the border, as well as far inland. Areas under consideration include Vyborg near the Finnish border; the districts of the Maritime Territory adjoining Nakhodka and Vladivostok and the Khasan district in the Far East; and Armenia and the Crimea in the south. The need to prevent the kind of uneven levels of development within the country that can be observed in the case of China has led Soviet reformers to consider the creation of SEZs 'not just in border districts but also in other regions of the country' such as Western Siberia.[32] The Vyborg zone, for example, is to be based in Leningrad, where it can draw on the rich pool of academic resources. It is hoped that joint ventures in that region will work mainly in the high-technology sphere, in the computer industry, and in research and development. Similar characteristics are envisaged in a planned technology park in Akademgorodok, noted for its concentration of academic researchers, near Novosibirsk. The SEZ in Nakhodka, by contrast, is to be based on the raw-materials processing industry. Birobidjan, in the Far East, will develop various industries in cooperation with Chinese neighbours, while Novgorod and Sochi will concentrate on tourism and tourist services. Owing to the rapidly deteriorating domestic economic situation, production facilities in SEZs, unlike those in China, will be encouraged to cater for the domestic market as well as for the export market.

Whatever the future economic character of the zones, they will most probably be granted preferential taxation and their own customs regimes (through a harmonized customs tariff), currency exchange laws, and foreign travel arrangements. There will have to be free movement of capital and people within the zones. They are also expected to be given much greater local economic autonomy. In most cases it will be up to local authorities in cooperation with domestic and foreign companies to develop the infrastructure and the economic base of their particular SEZ. Central government will be responsible only for general legislation and regulations, and will assist SEZs financially only where the work is of national importance (for instance, in building an airport or a major, strategically important, road).

In the Far East, taxation is lower and there are longer than usual tax exemption periods. In all border-trade regions, increased hard-currency exemptions for local authorities are permitted, and 'the entire amount of earnings from the export of goods within the framework of border and coastal trade shall remain at the disposal of the Council of Ministers of Union Republics, and territorial and regional executive committees for purchasing consumer goods, machines, equipment, primary goods and materials abroad'.[33]

Thus, in May 1990, the regional executive committee of Sakhalin Oblast (region) was designated a Free Enterprise Zone (FEZ), a new category designed to make the transition to a free market economy. Two months later, in July, Vladivostok followed suit and also became a FEZ.[34] A fund, open to foreign participation, has been set up to promote Sakhalin's socio-economic development and to assist in the 'training of cadres capable of operating in market conditions'.[35] The Sakhalin Foundation will not pay interest on deposits, but participants will be given preferential treatment in placing capital investment in the Oblast. The FEZ is seen to differ from SEZs in so far as it emphasizes changes to the local economy as a whole, not just means of encouraging foreign investment. The FEZ, which is being promoted by Valentin Fedorov,† the newly elected Chairman of the Sakhalin Oblast and the Kurile Islands, envisages free competition among state enterprises, joint-stock companies and JVs with foreign firms, a stock exchange, and competing banks. It is planned to introduce a convertible rouble, sell land to individuals and permit private enterprises to hire labour. According to unofficial reports, more progress along the same lines is to be expected in other areas in 1990–1.

Joint ventures in practice

The assessment given so far demonstrates the speed with which the JV policy has progressed. Table 4.3 shows the dynamics of this progress and its likely future development. The figures in the table also illustrate the changing share of foreign participation, which is directly related to the evolving pattern of legislation.

By the end of 1988, in terms of foundation capital, JVs with five foreign countries accounted for 54.6% of the total (see Table 4.4), and the leading Western partners, in terms of investment, were Italy, West Germany, Austria, France and Finland. As Table 4.4 illustrates, the total initial capital invested does not necessarily correspond to the number of JVs concluded. Thus JVs with Italy have the largest foundation capital, although Italy participates in only 17 JVs, behind West Germany with 29 JVs, and Finland with 27.

It should be noted that West Germany, Finland and Italy are also the top three Soviet foreign trade partners among the Western countries. Austria, however, which occupied the ninth place in terms of trade turnover with the USSR (R1.031bn in 1987), stands out as a relatively more active participant in Soviet JVs than countries such as Japan, France, Great Britain, the USA or Belgium.[36]

Geographically, some 50% of JVs are located in Moscow, while 74.3% are located in the Russian Republic, followed by Estonia with 7.1% (see Table 4.5). The Ukraine and Latvia have increased their share in JV locations in 1989 as compared with 1988. Surprisingly, Lithuania, which was the most active in its political drive to secede from the USSR, has hampered the creation of JVs with foreign countries on its territory: its share declined from 2.1% in 1988 to 1.0% in 1989.

Sectoral distribution of joint ventures

An important change has occurred in the approach of Soviet planners to the types of activities that are regarded as suitable for JVs. Whereas the initial plan was to allow JVs in only high-priority sectors and on a limited scale, most branches of the economy are now covered, although the question of scale envisaged or numbers to be involved in each industry still remains unclear.

The involvement of foreign firms in hotel-building or technological cooperation is an established practice in the USSR, but at present JVs have been concluded in areas that for nearly six decades (since the end of the concessions in the 1920s) have been out of bounds for foreigners. These new areas include tourist services, sports facilities, food preparation and catering services, advertising, marketing, production of consumer goods, communications equipment, computers and software, and even the production of sports cars.[37]

By the beginning of 1989 manufacturing was the most capital-intensive branch: it accounted for 44% of all JVs set up (excluding those in the computer industry), and for 62.5% of total capital involved (see Table 4.6). Industries favoured are machine-building and wood, paper and paper products, followed by chemicals and chemical products, drugs, plastics and glass. By way of comparison, the average annual number of JVs in the manufacturing sector in the United States for the period 1966–79 was 52.5% of the total number of JVs.[38] The least capital-intensive branch is construction: it covers 5.2% of the number of JVs set up, but accounts for only 1.8% of the total capital. JVs in business and services account for 14.1%, but their capital is also small at 7.5% of the total. JVs in computing account for 16.2% (31) of the total number of JVs, and 10.4% of the total capital. The rest of the JVs are quite evenly distributed in other branches of the economy, except for the areas of electricity, gas and water (Major Division 4), where no JVs had been reported by the end of 1988.[39]

The rapid growth in the number of JVs set up in the Soviet Union indicates an increasing interest in the Soviet market on the part of foreign investors. By March 1990, no JVs had been formally closed down. At the same time, there are growing concerns for the further implementation of the reforms in the USSR, about the credit-worthiness of Soviet enterprises, and, most important, about the political stability of the country.[40] I shall deal further with these issues in the concluding chapter.

5

THE USSR AND INTERNATIONAL ORGANIZATIONS

In the postwar years, although it had participated in setting up the Bretton Woods system, the Soviet Union shunned international economic organizations such as GATT, the IMF, the World Bank and the EEC. For its part, the West opposed Soviet participation. Now, however, Soviet policy towards international economic institutions is undergoing a transformation as part of the general change of course described in earlier chapters. The USSR wants to become a part of the successful developed Western world. In this chapter, I shall discuss Soviet relations with some of the major international economic organizations, and the possible costs and benefits of the emerging policy.

The General Agreement on Tariffs and Trade

The General Agreement on Tariffs and Trade (GATT) serves as a major framework for international trade. By October 1989 there were 97 contracting parties to GATT, of which 72 were members of the GATT Council. In addition, 58 countries have observer status. Observers may be present at the work of GATT Council, committees and negotiation sessions; they may conduct consultations with the GATT secretariat and with the contracting parties, and may avail themselves of information and advisory services provided by GATT, but they may not vote or have any active role in its proceedings. The contracting parties and the observers together account for some 90% of world trade. The aim of GATT is to promote free and fair international trade, by the reduction of tariffs and other restrictive measures.[1]

In 1986, the Soviet Union declared its intention of joint GATT, which it viewed as a positive organization, and, in August 1986, officially applied to participate in GATT talks, in the Uruguay Round. At a meeting of the Joint Soviet-American Commercial Commission that took place in Washington in December 1986, the Soviet delegation stated that the Soviet Union wished eventually to join GATT as a contracting party on agreed terms, but at the intermediate stage was interested only in obtaining observer status. It also stated that 'the Soviet side was prepared to observe the relevant rules, procedures and traditions of GATT, and after joining it – the treaty obligations'.[2] Of course, observer status does not automatically imply a move to full membership in the future, although this has been the usual practice so far. The majority of GATT members, however, resisted this first Soviet attempt. The state-run Soviet command economy was considered to be incompatible with GATT principles. It was argued that, because of the large size of the Soviet economy and its share in world trade, the accession of the still unreformed Soviet Union (unlike that of Poland or Hungary) could obstruct and even cripple the work of GATT, which in any case was preoccupied by the late 1980s with the negotiations of the Uruguay Round.[3]

However, progress continued to be made in economic legislation, East-West relations improved further, and Moscow secured the support, for its application to GATT, of the US President, in Malta in December 1989, and of the European Council, at Strasbourg on 8–9 December 1989. At the beginning of March 1990, the Soviet Union again formally applied for observer status in GATT, and was admitted on 16 May 1990.

Motives

Gorbachev explained the Soviet approach to GATT in an interview in *L'Unita*, published in May 1987: 'It is one of those international mechanisms which can and, we believe, must be used to unite the efforts of all countries in the task of improving world economic relations. Hence our interest in GATT and in the multilateral trade talks being held within its framework.'[4]

The motives behind the Soviet application to join GATT are related both to foreign and to domestic policy. Internationally, membership of GATT would allow the USSR to benefit from non-discrimination in foreign trade with Western countries; to gain a greater measure of acceptance and legitimacy as an international trading partner; and to exert more influence on the conduct of international trade. Domestically, it could overcome resistance to economic liberalization, and induce industry to improve its performance in terms of quality, efficiency and competitiveness. Indeed, the domestic aspect is considered by some Soviet specialists to be the more important of the two.[5]

Benefits

The possible impact of the Soviet change in attitude towards GATT is likely to be many-sided. The USSR may indeed play a more prominent role in global international trade policy. Exposure to increased competition will inject greater vigour into the programme for raising Soviet industrial production to internationally accepted quality and efficiency standards. This in turn should improve its trade structure. These benefits, however, will not come at once. Their achievement will take more than one decade, even if there is progress towards market economy, price reform, rouble convertibility, and transparency of domestic and foreign economic legislation and practice. All of the above measures are unlikely to be completed before the year 2000, and may easily take until 2010. Only after then will full membership in GATT become a serious prospect for the USSR. This does not mean, of course, that the USSR cannot benefit from observer status at GATT. Indeed, the country can now learn at first hand about the workings of GATT, about its requirements and benefits, as well as about the difficulties it faces. Meanwhile, the USSR will benefit from better information on the trade policies of the other GATT members, and in other secondary ways.

Costs

Soviet participation in GATT would undoubtedly place the country in a difficult situation because of the competition it would face from the more developed countries. The Soviet Union would be expected to provide the necessary and internationally accepted information and statistics about its economic performance and about its internal and external debt. It would also be expected to cut government subsidies, to introduce a price reform, and to abstain from dumping practices. At present, for example, a Zhiguli/Lada car is sold in the USSR at R8,600 (official price; the free market price would be R16,000), while an upgraded model of the same car costs £3,333 in the UK, and that is at the official commercial rouble/pound exchange rate of about 1:1. If, however, we applied the tourist rate of exchange of 10:1, which is less than half of the black-market rate, the UK price should be £860 per car. This clearly demonstrates the absurdity of the Soviet price system. The differentiated currency coefficients (DCCs) or multiple exchange rates, of which some 3,000 are in existence at present, would have to be abandoned in favour of a single realistic exchange rate. Government subsidies would have to be dropped as well. There would be no discrimination against or impediments to the sale of foreign goods on the domestic market,[6] and all quantitative import and export restrictions would have to be lifted. State trading would have to be conducted in accordance with commercial considerations.

The Soviet foreign economic legislation is to be amended to accommodate the necessary policy changes. Thus, for example, by 1991, work on a customs tariff system is to be completed. According to one Soviet author, it could take up to the year 2005 to implement the other legal measures needed in order to conform to GATT over such matters as the licensing system, quantitative export/import regulation, border equalizing taxation, participation in government purchases by foreign firms, a flexible system of export and import bans, import deposits, regulations on technical barriers in trade, the system of decreed minimum and maximum prices, and seasonal tariffs and tariff quotas for farm produce.[7] Soviet reformers, however, are convinced that the benefits of joining GATT are far greater than the costs.[8]

Impact on GATT
The pessimistic view expressed by some Western authors in the past

that the accession of the USSR to GATT might intensify the present deterioration of the organization, 'leaving the USSR with a Pyrrhic victory', is no longer held by Western governments.[9] The Uruguay Round is not expected to fail, nor is the USSR under perestroika expected to use GATT for making political mischief. Providing the USSR is successful in moving towards restructuring its economic and political system, its participation in GATT will serve as a confidence-building measure in relations between the USSR and the rest of the international community.

The Asian Development Bank

In 1987 a similarly positive stance was taken by Moscow towards the Manila-based Asian Development Bank (ADB). Created in 1966, the ADB has 47 member countries, 32 from the Asia-Pacific region, and 15 from Europe and North America.[10] The bank provides loans, technical assistance and advisory services, makes equity investments, and coordinates development policies. Soviet observers participated in the April 1987 meeting of the bank and also in its 1988 meeting in Manila.[11] Soviet membership of the ADB would provide the country with an additional source of finance and commercial expertise. It would also facilitate a more active participation in the Far Eastern markets.

The International Monetary Fund

The International Monetary Fund (IMF) was established as a specialized agency of the United Nations in 1945 under the Bretton Woods Agreements of 1944, and now has a membership of 152 nations. Its aims are to encourage stability of exchange, to promote a multilateral system of payments for current transactions between members, and to eliminate unnecessary foreign-exchange restrictions that may obstruct international commerce. Its functions include the provision of credits to nations (governments) experiencing balance-of-payments disequilibria, the provision of resources to finance export shortfalls and excesses in the cost of cereal imports, and contributions to international buffer stocks. The quotas, or capital subscriptions, of its members are the IMF's main source of lendable resources. These quotas may be reviewed once every five years, and altered with the consent of at least 85% of members. The amounts contributed by individual countries are broadly related to their economic size, and in 1985 totalled SDR 90bn. A member country has to invest 25% of its quota in reserve (hard) currency and 75% in its domestic currency.

The IMF is governed by an Executive Board, which consists of 22 Executive Directors. Only seven countries have their own seat on the board (the USA, the UK, the FRG, France, Japan, China and Saudi Arabia),[12] while the rest are divided into 15 groups with an elected director for each.

Although entry to GATT appeared on the agenda of Soviet foreign policy in 1986, the IMF was still viewed with considerable hostility as late as 1988.[13] In the spring of 1989 Ivan Ivanov was still arguing against a hasty application to join the IMF, on the grounds that 'a situation can result where we will share responsibility for IMF policies without being able to influence them'.[14] At present the USSR is considering joining both the IMF and the World Bank (discussed below),[15] although neither of these organizations allows observer status, so full membership would be necessary. Joining the IMF would enhance Soviet credibility in the world's financial markets and increase its prestige in the eyes of its commercial partners. It would improve its credit standing in the eyes of commercial banks. Other important benefits of being a member of the IMF are the availability of short-term credits (because drawings can be a multiple of quota), and the opportunity to exercise more influence on international monetary policies. The Soviet Union would have access to the detailed information bank on Fund members and on their economic performance, and to the analyses carried out by the Fund's staff.

Soviet experts estimate that the USSR's contribution to the fund would be between $800m and $900m and between R1.5b and R2b.[16] This relatively small contribution (about half the UK share) would place the USSR in the position of a medium-sized participant, and would not entitle it to a separate seat on the IMF Executive Board, unless it were given special treatment owing to its size and political weight, as is the case with China. As a member, it would (under current rules) be able to draw 110% of its quota in the first year, and up to a maximum of 330% of its quota for a three-year stand-by or Extended Fund Facility (EFF)* arrangement to a cumulative limit of 440%, and up to another 122% under the compensatory and contingency financing facility to offset external shocks (actual access would, however, probably be considerably more limited than this).[17]

Admitting the USSR to the IMF would be a major event not just for the USSR but for all the member countries. In practice it would be an irreversible step, since an overwhelming majority of votes – 85% – is needed to expel a member (this has happened only once, in 1954, in the case of Czechoslovakia). It is no wonder, therefore, that the member countries are cautious. They want to make sure that, once admitted, the Soviet Union will fully comply with the rules of the IMF, and that it will not try to exert undue pressure on the other members or to politicize the organization, as was the case with the United Nations.

The World Bank

Membership of the IMF will qualify the Soviet Union to join the International Bank for Reconstruction and Development (IBRD), or World Bank, as it is more commonly known. This was established in December 1945, and also administers the International Development Association (IDA), set up in September 1960. The IBRD has 152 member countries. The IDA has a membership of 137, and provides assistance chiefly to the poorer developing countries. The Bank also provides credits and advice, but only to developing countries. Between 75% and 80% of its lending is strictly project-related.

The World Bank also set up, in April 1988, the Multilateral Investment Guarantee Agency (MIGA) with the aim of supplementing national investment guarantee schemes and private political risk insurance. It provides guarantees against currency transfer, expropriation, war, revolution or civil disturbance, and breach of contract

---

* The EFF, established in 1974, is used in connection with balance-of-payments difficulties. It is designed to provide members with the financial support they need over a period (normally three years) which is long enough to permit them to implement suitable corrective policies.

risks, as well as offering advisory services to developing members as a means of improving their foreign investment climate. The agency guarantees up to 90% of an investment up to a limit of $50m per project.

Another World-Bank-related agency is the Foreign Investment Advisory Service (FIAS), which is a joint venture between MIGA and the World Bank's International Finance Corporation (IFC). By mid-1990 the FIAS was active in 25 countries in assisting governments to develop investment laws, policies and programmes, and institutions that promote and regulate foreign investment. The FIAS helped China to draft its joint venture laws. Countries such as Indonesia, Chile and Togo have also benefited from the service.[18]

Whether the Soviet Union should join the World Bank as a donor or as a borrower is at present a matter for debate. In mid-1990 the maximum GNP per capita for a borrower nation stood at $3,800 (in 1988 US dollars). Some Western specialists argue that the Soviet Union should be admitted as a donor nation, since it would otherwise compete with many weaker nations for the World Bank's limited resources, while political backing for the World Bank by developed countries could be weakened if the USSR were a major borrower.[19] The problem, however, is not just one of politics but also one of estimating the real value of Soviet GNP. Because of the deformed price structure in the USSR it is impossible to calculate its real GNP with certainty. The present estimates of Soviet GNP vary between $2,012bn ($7,085 per capita, using 1987 figures in 1982 US dollars), if Soviet GNP is taken as 53% of that of the USA,[20] and $949bn ($3,342 per capita), if it is just 25% of the US GNP.[21] The lower figure seems to be closer to reality. If it were accepted it would place the Soviet Union in the borrower category. For the Soviet Union to be accepted as a borrower, however, it would have substantially to reduce its economic and military aid to Third World countries, such as Cuba, Vietnam and North Korea, and whether it would be prepared to do this is a matter of doubt.

Aid places a heavy financial burden on the USSR: it accounted for 1.3% of the country's GNP in the early 1980s. At the same time the figure was 0.2% for the US and 0.4% for the UK. By 1986 it had risen to 1.7% in the USSR, while Soviet export credits to Third

World countries amounted to $60bn.[22] According to CIA estimates, the USSR extended aid amounting to $15.7bn to less developed countries in the four-year period 1985–8, while arms deliveries came to $68.4bn (making a total of $84.1bn) (see Table A3 in Appendix 6).[23] According to Soviet sources, the state budget for 1989 provided for R12.5bn ($20.3bn) of state credits and irrecoverable aid to foreign countries. This accounted for 1.4% of Soviet GNP of R900bn ($1,458bn). In 1990 this sum was reduced to R9.7bn ($15.7bn). However, the overall debt owed to the USSR by the recipients of Soviet aid amounted to R85.8bn ($139.1bn) by November 1989. In contrast, Soviet debt to foreign countries at the beginning of the same year was R33.6bn ($54.4bn).[24]

There are signs that the USSR may now be ready to alter its position as a global superpower.[25] Being able to offer practical aid to its allies will, however, remain a matter of political and military importance. It is likely that aid packages will be trimmed, as happened with Soviet aid to Eastern Europe, but doubtful whether they will be abandoned, just for the benefit of becoming a World Bank borrower. If this assumption is correct, then Soviet membership of the World Bank will be mainly of a political and information-gathering nature. It is also possible, however, that economic realities will force the USSR to make the necessary cuts, and acquire borrower status.

The European Bank for Reconstruction and Development
The EBRD was created in May 1990 to help economic restructuring and recovery in the re-emerging democracies in Eastern Europe. It will be based in London. The bank has 42 members: all the European countries (except Albania), the United States, Canada, Mexico, Japan, Australia, New Zealand, South Korea, Egypt, Morocco, Israel, and two institutions – the EEC and the European Investment Bank. The EBRD's initial capital is to be 10bn ecus (around $12bn or £7.2bn) supplied by governments and by the private sector. The 12 members of the EC and its institutions will hold 53.7% of the new bank's capital. Britain, West Germany, France, Italy and Japan will each have 8.5%, while the United States

will have the biggest share – 10%. The bank's activities will be aimed primarily at the private sector. No more than 40% of its loans will be committed to the state sector, while state-owned enterprises will be able to get funds only if they adopt free-market strategies.[26] The EBRD will be expected to complement the activities of the IMF and the World Bank in developing special expertise and credit facilities in order to enhance Western economic support to the East European countries.

The initial opposition, mainly on political grounds, of the US and Japan to Soviet participation in the bank subsided in the face of arguments to the contrary put by France and other countries. France proposed that the Soviet Union should be allowed an 8% share in the bank's initial capital, but eventually it received a 6% stake (600m ecus).[27] The actual Soviet contribution to the bank, however, will amount for the first three years to only 30% of quota (180m ecus or £135m). On US insistence, moreover, the Soviet Union has agreed not to borrow more than its paid-in contribution during the first three years. The EBRD will be the first international financial institution to have the Soviet Union as a member. This means that Soviet entry for the time being has greater political than economic significance, but should not obscure the fact that the Soviet Union will derive important benefits from its access to the EBRD's expertise, information and advice. The initial low financial profile, combined with close cooperation in the other spheres of the bank's activity, may indeed be a useful transitional arrangement.

The European Community
Before 1975, the EC was treated by the Soviet Union as an aggressive and anti-Soviet economic alliance, whose existence was barely recognized. However, in the period 1977–81, following the Helsinki Accords, contacts took place between the CMEA and the EC in an effort to achieve mutual recognition. Progress was blocked by the USSR's refusal to countenance the setting up of direct relations between individual East European states and Brussels. The talks were broken off as a result of the cooling in East-West relations at the end of the 1970s. Only in June 1985, in one of the first

measures implementing 'new political thinking', did the Soviet Union request the resumption of CMEA talks with the EC, having reversed its position so as to open the way to bilateral ties between the EC and separate countries in Eastern Europe.

On 25 July 1988, the foreign ministers of the 12 member countries of the EC gave the green light to opening discussions with the USSR on a far-reaching economic cooperation agreement. They also agreed that the EC as a bloc should for the first time discuss foreign policy issues with the Soviet Union. A year and a half later, on 18 December 1989, the USSR signed a substantial agreement with the EC and the European Atomic Energy Community (EAEC) concerning trade, and commercial and economic cooperation. The ten-year agreement provides for MFN status in trade for both sides. The EC is to abolish progressively some 1,300 quantitative restrictions on imports from the USSR before 1995 (600 of these within the first year).[28] The agreement replaces 12 previous bilateral trade deals with the member states, to be nullified by the EC in 1992.[29]

The USSR has undertaken to grant EC imports non-discriminatory treatment concerning quantitative restrictions, the granting of licences and the allocation of currency needed to pay for these imports. EC businessmen working in the USSR will also be treated in a non-discriminatory way.

In addition to the above framework agreement, a complementary sectoral agreement concerning trade in textiles has been discussed. The framework agreement is being seen by the Soviet side as a major step towards closer cooperation with the West European countries, lessening discrimination, weakening the application of the CoCom regulations, accepting GATT practices, and encouraging restructuring of the Soviet foreign economic apparatus.[30]

6

CONCLUSION

There is no guarantee that the policy of perestroika will proceed smoothly – conservatism is deeply rooted in Soviet society. Yanov's warning of the possibility of a right-wing counter-reform should be taken seriously. However, the elements of a deep positive change are in evidence. Thus the policy of glasnost provides a mechanism for informing the public and for criticizing the government and the party bureaucracy that has had far-reaching and irreversible effects. Democratization of public institutions and the growth of political pluralism are having profound consequences. The developing unconstrained contacts with the outside world are increasing the level of mutual understanding and tolerance. Widening East-West cooperation and Western participation in the Soviet economy can play an important part in shaping the future development of the USSR.

During the New Economic Policy of the 1920s the Bolshevik ideology was altered slightly to accommodate immediate needs, but was never discarded. As a result, NEP could be abandoned almost as soon as it appeared. This time the ideological revision is much deeper than at any time in the past. The accompanying change in policies and actions are thus more likely to be of a strategic and long-term kind: indeed, a revolutionary change may be under way. Certainly the traditional Soviet conception of an irreconcilable ideological and military struggle with the West has been abandoned, drawing the Soviet Union closer to Western values and thereby helping to normalize relations between East and West. With perestroika, 'merchant' attitudes are manifest concurrently in both foreign and domestic policy.

This concluding chapter identifies the obstacles that lie in the path of the overall reform programme, assesses the progress that has been made in reforming foreign economic policy, and suggests proposals for further change.

Problems facing the Soviet reform programme

Foreign economic policy is not autonomous: it operates in close connection with other spheres of political and economic activity. Its fate, as we have seen, is intertwined with the reform programme generally. The current reform prospect faces serious problems in economic, social, political, ethnic and ecological spheres. Among the challenges in foreign affairs are those associated with the areas of security, international economy, international politics and the global environment.

Domestic economic aspects

Initiating the reform process in the second half of the 1980s, the Soviet leadership started the process of dismantling the old centralized economic system, but five years later it had not been able or, to be more precise, willing to replace it by an effective market-based system. By mid-1990 the Gorbachev government was referring to the future Soviet economy as a 'regulated market economy' – neither a capitalist nor a socialist one, but a third variety. It is a matter of broad consensus among economists in the West, however, that there is no viable 'third way'. The empirical evidence available so far seems to support this assessment. Meanwhile, tinkering with the system has inevitably led to increasing destabilization of the economy, disruption of the supply system, disappearance of consumer goods and foodstuffs from the shops, and to increased levels of corruption, racketeering and violent crime. It is becoming more and more evident that perestroika, in the sense of reforming an existing system, has exhausted itself. Radicals argue, with justice, that only a decisive revolutionary change to a capitalist type of economy can save the situation.

Specific economic problems include disequilibrium in household income and outlay arising from suppressed inflation. Money in savings accounts amounted to R337bn in 1989 and it is estimated that a similar amount had been accumulated outside the officially monitored system.[1] The budget deficit, at between 11% and 14% of GNP, is very high (in the US it is about 3%). Inflation is becoming overt, and is estimated to be between 10% and 30% annually, depending on economic sector. The rouble is, in effect, not convertible either into goods (most tradable goods are scarce and not readily available for purchase) or into foreign currency (it is not accepted abroad, and hard currency may not be freely purchased domestically), hindering commercial relations inside the country and with the outside world.

Under Gorbachev the traditional communist attitude towards money as simply an accounting unit has changed. However, because of the problems outlined above, the difficulties that stand in the way of achieving convertibility of the rouble, and strengthening it against other currencies, are even greater now than in the past. If in the 1920s the gold standard could have been introduced with relative ease in a Soviet Russia rich in gold, in the 1980s it is more a question of the total strength of the economy. This means eliminating the shortage economy, with domestic prices reflecting domestic scarcities.

The Soviet economic infrastructure is run down and inefficient. Outside the main cities the quality of roads ranges from bad to impassable. The railway system is overloaded and does not cope well with the growing transportation needs of the economy, which also has an adverse effect on foreign trade. Moreover, Soviet railways have a different gauge from those in the West. This means that, to cross the border, goods often have to be reloaded, increasing the cost and time needed for delivery.[2]

The telephone network is antiquated. There is no direct dialling abroad from the USSR. It is not possible to have more than 68 simultaneous phone calls between the Soviet Union and Britain, including faxes, or more than 32 with the United States.[3] As a result it may take a whole working-day to make a phone call or to send a fax to the USSR from abroad. Even though the number of fax machines in the USSR is growing, a severe shortage of paper renders many machines useless.

Lastly, the lack of open information and reliable statistics has deprived Soviet citizens in general, and specialists in particular, of the information necessary for the normal and efficient functioning of a modern economy. This state of affairs can be remedied only slowly, and it represents a serious obstacle to the planning of reform.

Social aspects

Problems are being created by changes in the official attitude to property and ownership. After decades of a policy of relative egalitarianism, there is now a sharp shift in the balance from moral to material incentives, and greater readiness on the part of the reformist leadership to accept the inevitable social inequalities. The population, however, is used to reliance on the state for social security, health care, education and employment. The effect has been described as akin to that of living in a greenhouse. Now the social 'greenhouse' is being dismantled, and for many this is hard to accept. There is widespread criticism of the free-market cooperatives, although over four million people were involved in cooperative activity by the beginning of 1990. The fact that members of the cooperatives are paid more than the average wage creates feelings of envy and their activities are hampered by local officials. The general questioning of traditional values and of authority is held by some to be responsible for an increase in the crime rate. In 1989 it went up by 31.8%. In Leningrad in the first half of 1989, for example, muggings and thefts increased by 150%, car thefts by 100% and burglaries by 10%.[4]

The Soviet Union suffers from a major housing problem. By mid-1990 the queue for better housing stood at 14 million people, while some 4.5 million families had less than 55 square feet per person. Over 6 million people live in communal flats, where a kitchen and bathroom are shared among several families.[5] The shortage of housing and the rigidity of the housing market represent a substantial obstacle to the greater labour mobility that economic restructuring will require.

Encouraged by the growing freedom of expression and political activity, workers show their discontent with poor living conditions, and rationing of food and consumer goods by means of strikes and protests. According to Prime Minister Nikolai Ryzhkov, as many as 30,000 workers on average were on strike daily in 1989, while Deputy Prime Minister Leonid Abalkin has quoted a figure of 400,000 workers who were daily missing from work as a result of absenteeism, unplanned holidays and participation in social activities. It is estimated that as a result the Soviet economy lost more than 7.5 million work-days and R2bn worth of production.[6] Lately the situation has become even worse: in the first quarter of 1990 an average of 130,000 workers were on strike each day. At the same time, the absolute volume of industrial production has decreased by 1.2% as compared with the first quarter of 1989.[7] Such disruption is bound to increase if serious economic reforms are initiated. Opposition from trade unions is already being cited as a reason for caution with reform.

Political aspects

The CPSU is experiencing ever-growing pressure from different groups, inside and outside the party, to relinquish its monopoly of power and change its role and function. As a result of this pressure, fundamental changes in the political system seem to be under way. In 1990, the Congress of People's Deputies changed Article 6 of the 1977 constitution in order to permit a plurality of parties: the Communist Party's leading role is no longer specified. The contours of a new political system, however, are as yet far from clear, and the party apparatus continues to wield enormous power, often acting as a barrier to change.

Political challenges are also arising from the constituent republics, and these challenges are based on the national aspirations of their populations. These aspirations challenge the very existence of the Soviet Union within its present borders, and hence the integrity of the national market. They strengthen the position of hardliners, especially in the Russian Soviet Federal Socialist Republic, who argue that the reforms should be slowed down. This political disarray, and the loss of popular support which the government is currently suffering, will greatly complicate the task of developing a consistent economic policy, especially one that requires material sacrifices from numerous sections of the population. Paradoxically, democratization, now widely accepted as a precondition of economic reform, can end up hampering its implementation.

Comparing Soviet perestroika with the 'open door' policy in China reveals some basic differences in the reform processes in each country. China initiated its reform earlier than the USSR, but it did so only in the economic sphere, leaving politics relatively unchanged. At first the policy proved to be a success. It was only when political reforms were demanded by the student demonstrators that the reform process stalled. Soviet reformers also started perestroika largely with the economy in mind, but just three years later, in 1988, went ahead with political changes. The latter proved to be destabilizing. The extent of the pent-up anger and disappointment of 70 years was something that the reformers, apparently, had not taken into consideration. As a result, economic difficulties compounded by political demands from different quarters have raised the prospect of the disintegration of the Soviet system and of the Soviet state.

International economic aspects
The chief challenges faced by Soviet reformers in the international economic sphere include a highly sophisticated and competitive international market, CoCom regulations, and Soviet non-membership of international economic organizations and agreements, such as the World Bank, the IMF, GATT, and the International Labour Organizations. The Soviet government is accordingly striving to widen its participation in such institutions.

On the other hand, the growing trend towards economic interdependence in the Western world creates conditions favourable to reform in the USSR. FDI has increased considerably in the past decade. Thus, in the five years 1983–8, FDI by the G-5 (the USA, Japan, West Germany, France and the UK) grew by 30% annually in real terms, compared with growth in world trade of less than 5% per annum.[8] Economists predict that the global stock of FDI by 1995 will be at least 2.2 times the 1988 stock in real terms.[9] In the G-5, roughly four million industrial workers are employed by foreign-owned firms, representing 8% of total manufacturing employment. Western companies are looking for new sites for expansion, for new markets and for cheaper labour. These are all to be found in the USSR.

Ecological aspects

For decades the state of the country's environment received little or no consideration from the authorities. A study by the National Geographic Institute and the Academy of Sciences, which was published in 1989, classified 16% of the Soviet Union as an 'ecological disaster', in which 50 million people suffer the effects of industrial, chemical and nuclear pollution. No less than 42% of the total milk supply was polluted with chemicals. In Leningrad alone 30% of all food is dangerous to health, while 26% of the Soviet population live in 126 heavily polluted towns.[10] In 1988 the infant mortality rate for the country as a whole was 24.7 deaths per 1,000 births. By contrast, in Japan, Sweden and Finland the rate – up to the age of one year – is less than 6 deaths per 1,000 births.[11]

The indiscriminate use of pesticides and chemical fertilizers has resulted in serious damage to the health of large populations in the southern republics of Uzbekistan, Kazakhstan and Turkmenistan, and in the poisoning of the soil.[12] The Chernobyl accident of April 1986, its fall-out estimated to be 50 times greater than that of the Hiroshima atom bomb, had by 1990 resulted officially in at least 300 deaths (the true figure may be much higher), genetic abnormalities in humans and animals, and long-lasting contamination of vast agricultural areas.[13] It was estimated to have cost R80bn by the beginning of 1990.[14] That particular accident had an enormous impact on the leadership's thinking and perceptions about the Soviet economy. Zhores Medvedev goes so far as to argue that Chernobyl has precipitated an economic and political crisis in the Soviet Union and in the countries linked to it economically.[15]

Like the rest of the world, the USSR is faced with the problem of the deteriorating condition of the ozone layer, and the phenomenon of acid rain. To combat all these ecological and environmental challenges the country needs large-scale additional investment in industry, agriculture and health care. The necessary resources will be in short supply.

Progress so far
We have seen how different domestic and external factors have worked to precipitate reform in the Soviet Union. The country had reached a situation in which the oligarchy were unable to rule in the old way, and the ruled were unwilling to live under the old conditions. A major transformation thus became inevitable. The initial partial reforms in economic policy, however, could not and did not produce the hoped-for results.

Five years on, the organizational, political, domestic, and international economic and ecological difficulties that perestroika encountered in its early years have been transformed to varying degrees. Problems associated with international economic aspects have been receding. The disarmament process has accelerated, NATO has revised its assessment of the Soviet threat, and the Warsaw Pact is in the process of disintegration. Domestically, the Soviet Union is also going through a liberalizing process in both politics and the economy. At the same time – because of inherited systemic problems, ideological rigidity, and political shortsightedness and indecision – the economy has been destabilized during the first five years of perestroika to such an extent that the country is on the verge of economic collapse. With increasing unemployment, a rising crime rate, inter-ethnic violence and the growing number of internal refugees, the social problems are approaching boiling-point. The ecological mismanagement of the past is starting to levy its charge on the present generation. The situation contains the potential both for a radicalization of the reform process and for an attempt to restore order along the old lines.

Opposing views and institutional interests have clashed on the issue of opening up towards the outside world. The debate concerning the conduct of foreign economic policy revolves around the issue of monopolistic state management as against foreign participation through JVs in the running of the domestic economy. The debate – which touches upon the emotionally explosive issue of 'selling out mother Russia to foreigners', on the right to private property, on the notion of egalitarianism, and generally on the acceptability of a market economy – has not been unequivocally resolved, and will probably continue for years to come.

Between 1986 and 1988, foreign economic legislation advanced considerably in the direction of decentralization and demonopolization. As early as the spring of 1989, however, a process of export-import licensing had started to impede foreign trade activity. With the deteriorating internal economic situation the licensing policy became even harsher by the end of that year. The close relationship between the domestic factors and foreign economic policy means that lack of progress in economic reform has turned out to be an obstacle to developing new types of external economic relations.

The commodity structure of Soviet foreign trade has remained unchanged since the beginning of perestroika. Altering this is the most difficult task facing foreign economic policy. It is relatively easy to export raw materials, but much harder to produce high-quality finished goods which can compete successfully on the world market. Similarly, the efficiency of agricultural production cannot be boosted overnight: grain imports will have to continue for the foreseeable future. Nor will the transfer to hard-currency settlements between the USSR and the East European countries bring about a rapid change in the trading patterns of the two sides. The East European countries depend on Soviet energy supplies, while the Soviet Union is the chief market for the export of low-quality East European consumer goods. The infrastructure for oil and gas deliveries is in place, and the Soviet side may well be prepared to continue offering concessionary prices. It is widely accepted that even for East Germany, which will enjoy massive financial and technological support from West Germany, the transition to West European standards, quality and efficiency may take at least five years.

Apart from the process of decentralization and demonopolization, the key feature of economic reform is the opening-up of the domestic economy to JVs with foreign firms. The number of JVs registered is growing steadily, and so is the amount of foreign capital involved. JVs function in the still largely unreformed, domestic economic environment, which makes progress difficult. It is even possible that, with the mounting difficulties, restrictions and limitations on the existing JV legislation will be imposed in the near future.

It is still too early to look for any practical results from JV policy, since most of the businesses concerned are still being set up. Any impact on Soviet economic performance at home and abroad cannot be expected to materialize before the mid-1990s.

The Soviet attitude towards international organizations has shifted dramatically. The establishment of normal relations with the EC and observer status in GATT are important milestones towards reincorporation into the world economy. Membership of EBRD is another step towards joining the IMF and the Bank. These stages of rapprochement between the Soviet Union and the Western world are expressions of a profound strategic turnabout in Soviet policy and of recognition of this change on the part of the outside world.

The future

In a fast-changing political and economic environment, it is difficult to predict the future of the Soviet policy of reform. Broadly, we may consider three possible options for the future of Soviet foreign economic policy, which depend on the general development of the reform: (a) radical-liberal; (b) conservative-regressive; (c) intermediate (a mix of (a) and (b)). These options follow from the views, discussed in Chapter 2, of the participants in the ongoing debate about perestroika. The Western response to perestroika, considered below, will largely depend on which one of the above options prevails.

The first option implies a decisive shift towards a free-market economy, combined with a determined policy pushing for export-led growth, demonopolization and denationalization of the economy, rouble convertibility, a major reduction in the defence budget and the conversion of military industry to civilian production, opening up the Soviet economy to foreign business and close cooperation with international economic organizations. Such trends are visible in 1990 in East Germany, Poland, Czechoslovakia and Hungary.

The second option implies a return to the old Stalinist method of tight centralized control of the economy, tight central planning, non-cooperation with the Western countries and non-participation in international economic organizations, while retaining a one-party system. This option is reminiscent of the termination of NEP in the late 1920s and early 1930s.

Both options (a) and (b) are, of course, extreme examples. Nevertheless, history demonstrates that neither can be entirely ruled out as a possibility. The Soviet Union, however, is a large and complex state with a politically and economically awakening society. It contains at present certain groups favouring the first option. But the most likely outcome will be option (c), a mixture of the first and second options with the radical-liberal element preponderant.

The key to the future course of Soviet foreign economic policy is clearly to be found in the degree of success of domestic perestroika. This in turn depends on the ability of the government to oversee the necessary systemic transition from the centrally run Soviet-type economy to a market economy. It has to convince the population of the need for major unpopular measures, such as increased prices, monetary reform, private ownership of the means of production, abolition of subsidies, growing differentiation of incomes, and the abolition of guaranteed employment. Not much progress had been made in this direction by mid-1990. On 13 June 1990, frustrated by growing economic difficulties and the government's indecision in introducing a radical reform, the Supreme Soviet called on Gorbachev to use his power of presidential decree to denationalize state property, establish joint stock companies and a stock exchange, introduce anti-monopoly controls, reform the banking system and give new legal backing to small businesses and entrepreneurs.

All these are fundamental changes which would undoubtedly facilitate an improvement in conditions for Soviet foreign economic policy. Yet such radical measures will not be easily accepted by large segments of Soviet population. Matters are complicated by pressures for secession and greater autonomy, particularly in economic policy-making, from the constituent republics of the USSR. It will take many years before mutually acceptable solutions can be reached to the disputes between the numerous ethnic groups which inhabit the USSR. In the meantime, quite apart from the great political uncertainty and disruption that they cause, they pose enormous problems for the advancement of a coherent economic policy for the USSR as a whole.

In the case of the Baltic republics there seems a real possibility of independence in the near future. All three republics are self-sufficient in agricultural products, but have hardly any natural resources. Some 90% of raw materials and energy are imported from the other Soviet republics. It is clearly desirable from an economic point of view that the process of secession should be conducted in agreement with the USSR. A peaceful resolution of this matter is also desirable for the progress of Soviet foreign economic cooperation with the West. Thus, for example, in the summer of 1990 the US was reluctant to grant MFN status to the USSR because of the Soviet economic blockade of Lithuania, as well as the obstacles still being raised to Jewish emigration.

The continuing trend towards domestic economic decentralization will also result in regionalization of foreign economic activity. This may already be observed in the cases of the different republics, in expanding border trade, and, for example, in the existence of the FEZ in Sakhalin, or the proposed special economic zone in Vyborg. Local authorities will have much more autonomy in the conduct of their relations with the outside world. This liberalization will provide more opportunities for business promotion, but at the same time, owing to the diversity of regulations and specific local laws, may complicate the commercial environment still further. Because of increasing shortages, further export and import restrictions will be enforced, liberal foreign economic legislation will be reversed, more enterprises will become insolvent, and the government will be unwilling or unable to bail them out. The costs of doing business with the USSR will grow.

The break-up of the alliance with Eastern Europe means that in the long run economic relations with the CMEA countries will also be transformed. With the transition to hard-currency settlements starting in 1991, both the USSR and the East European countries will be looking to expand their trade relations with the Western countries and the NICs. Trade flows within the CMEA, however, will not change suddenly, because of the established economic interdependence between the USSR and the East European countries. From 1991 the USSR will have to be paid in hard currency for its oil and gas deliveries. It is doubtful whether the East European countries, apart from East Germany – which will then be part of the FRG – will in the medium term command the necessary amount of hard currency to do so. This will leave them with the old option of barter trade with the USSR, which is one of the few markets for their cheap consumer goods. On the other hand, the Soviet Union will have an interest in continuing to supply its East European neighbours: the trade relationship provides it with size-able economic and political leverage.

If West Germany is the main Soviet trade partner among Western countries (accounting for 18.2% in 1988), East Germany (with 18%) was the main one among the CMEA member countries. Together they account for just over 15% of total Soviet foreign trade. West Germany is also the leader in the number of JVs in the Soviet Union. The united Germany, to be formed on 3 October 1990, will be the single largest Soviet foreign trade partner, and will undoubtedly continue to be so.

If progress in reforming foreign economic relations depends on the success of domestic economic reform, external factors also affect the internal reform process. The Soviet Union's foreign economic policy must be more advanced than its domestic policy. It must permit the highest degree of foreign participation in the domestic reform process, including foreign ownership of the means of produc-tion in the USSR, free competition and non-discrimination. This will inevitably lead to some loss of sovereignty, because the Soviet government will no longer be able directly to command the country's entire economic activity. It will also have to comply with the requirements of the international economic organizations con-cerning the conduct of its domestic economy and to provide the necessary information and statistics. At the same time a policy of opening-up would inject Western know-how, vitality, commercial competition and higher industrial standards.

To judge by the Chinese experience of the past decade, if present trends to liberalize and decentralize the Soviet domestic economy and its foreign economic relations continue, the influence of joint ventures on Soviet technological progress and general economic performance is bound to be more important than the effect of imports or licensing arrangements could have been.[16] The number of JVs may reach 20,000 by the end of the decade, while foreign investment in JVs could amount to US\$25–30bn. This will help to overcome the economic inertia that has accumulated during the decades of command-economy rule.

The likely Western response

I have concluded that the most probable option for perestroika is radical-liberal rather than conservative. Contrary to some claims that the West is slow to respond to perestroika, there is a considerable shift in Western policies towards the USSR. We have already witnessed the conclusion of major East-West disarmament agreements, the virtual demise of the Warsaw Pact, and reassessments within NATO. CoCom restrictions are being downgraded, foreign participation in JVs in the USSR grows, and international economic organizations are opening their doors to Soviet participation.

It is often argued that the West cannot do much to influence Soviet reform. This is true to the extent that aid on the scale of the Marshall Plan is not likely, since the problem the Soviet Union faces is not just that of economic reconstruction but one of systemic, ideological reorientation.[17] One Soviet author, who favours increased Soviet borrowing in the West, estimated at the beginning of 1990 that the USSR needs R150–200bn (\$243–324bn) of additional capital, which could come from both internal and foreign sources, to help it to complete the transitional stage of perestroika.[18] However, if the West German aid of DM115bn pledged for the reconstruction of East Germany – the most industrially advanced among the East European countries – is taken as a rough indicator of what would be needed for the USSR's economic reconstruction, the required sum could be around DM2,223bn ($1,315bn).[19] Even with the best of intentions, no international agency or group of countries would be able to come up with such an immense amount. The USSR is not just the largest country; it is also the richest country in the world in terms of its natural resources. It has a fully literate population and a good science base, and, with an increase in industrial efficiency and a more coherent economic policy, these may considerably improve its foreign economic performance. However, both political and economic reforms are still inconclusive. Aid, therefore, would have to be targeted on areas such as training, technical assistance, technology transfer facilitated by the reduction of the CoCom list, institution-building, economic policy, and management advice and financial assistance for specific projects, the implementation of which should be monitored by the provider of aid.

The analysis presented in Chapter 4 shows that investment in the Soviet Union can be profitable, but it also may be hazardous, especially for those uninformed about the local conditions. As the experience of delayed payments to foreign firms early in 1990 showed, it remains a high-risk investment area. Alongside decisions made by Western governments, private investment decisions will be crucial to the degree to which the Soviet Union becomes integrated into the world economy. Much will depend on how far progress in the economy and the reform in general creates an attractive commercial and legal environment. Matters are also bound to be affected by broader changes in political relations between the USSR and the outside world, and by changes in the world economy. Investors will pay close attention to the precedents offered by the experience of China, Hungary and Poland.

It would be sensible, therefore, to take every possible precaution and insurance against any unexpected economic or political developments (including expropriation). All the above may be carried out by international bodies, such as the World Bank's Multilateral Investment Guarantee Agency and the International Finance Corporation, by private and government agencies such as the Overseas Private Investment Corporation in the US, by the Export Credits Guarantee Department in the UK, by Hermes in

West Germany and by other similar agencies. To enjoy the support of these, however, the USSR has to become a member of international economic organizations, such as the IMF and the World Bank, and, at a later stage, a full member of GATT.

The international organizations and agencies are usually complementary in their actions, and their work often overlaps. There may arise a problem of coordinating Western support to the Soviet Union and Eastern Europe. It has been suggested that responsibility for this could be taken on by the EC or the OECD.[20] Indeed, coordination is necessary, and, in the long term, it does not matter which particular organization emerges as the dominant one, so long as there is a coordinating mechanism. At the same time, excessively rigid coordination may prove to be counter-productive, since flexibility and a wider choice of policies would also be welcome. There is a great measure of goodwill towards the Soviet Union in the West. This goodwill, however, will bear fruit only if the Soviet Union starts to transform itself from within, if it discards compromised old dogmas, if it is willing to learn from the experience of others, and if it becomes a genuine democracy and an open society.

NOTES

Chapter 1

1 V. I. Lenin, *Sochineniya*, vol. 22, p. 108, in E. H. Carr, *The Bolshevik Revolution 1917–1923*, vol. 2 (Harmondsworth: Penguin Books, 1983), p. 81.
2 Karl Marx and Frederick Engels, *Manifesto of the Communist Party* (Beijing: Foreign Languages Press, 1975), pp. 59–60.
3 Carr, *The Bolshevik Revolution*, vol. 2, p. 131.
4 See 'Concerning Questions of the New Economic Policy and Industry', a resolution adopted on 28 December 1921, at the IX All-Russian Congress of Soviets, in K.U. Chernenko and M. S. Smirtyukov (comps), *Resheniya Partii i Pravitel'stva po khozyaistvennym voprosam (1917-1967)*, vol. 1, Politizdat Moscow, 1967, pp. 279–80.
5 Joseph Stalin, *Economic Problems of Socialism in the USSR* (Moscow: Foreign Languages Publishing House, 1952), p. 35.
6 Marshal I. Goldman, 'Gorbachev, Turnaround CEO', *Harvard Business Review*, no. 3, May-June 1988, p. 108. For a comparison of resource intensity of East European economies and those of industrialized West for 1979–80, see Jan Winiecki, *Economic Prospects – East and West: A View from the East* (London: Centre for Research into Communist Economies, 1987), p. 17.
7 *Sotsialisticheskaya industriya*, 22 March 1983; Slyun'kov's speech at the Party Central Committee meeting on 6 June 1987, quoted in Akio Kawato, 'The Soviet Union: A Player in the World Economy?', in Tsuyoshi Hasegawa and Alex Pravda (eds), *Perestroika: Soviet Domestic and Foreign Policies* (London: RIIA/Sage, 1990), p. 124.
8 Nikolai Shmelev, 'Ekonomika i zdravyi smysl', *Znamya*, July 1988,

quoted in Anthony Jones and William Moskoff (eds), *Perestroika and the Economy: New Thinking in Soviet Economics* (Armonk, NY: M. E. Sharpe, Inc., 1989), p. 268.

9 I. Abakumov, 'Grain imports: now at the stage of addiction', *Izvestiya*, 21 May 1990 (morning edition).

10 Vadim Medvedev, 'K poznaniyu sotsializma', *Kommunist*, no. 17, 1988, pp. 17–18.

11 M. Gorbachev, *Perestroika* (London: Collins, 1987), p. 148.

12 Goldman, 'Gorbachev, Turnaround CEO', pp. 110–11.

13 Alexander Yanov, *The Russian Challenge and the Year 2000*, translated by Iden J. Rosenthal (Oxford and New York: Basil Blackwell, 1987), p. 15, n. 15.

Chapter 2

1 See Gosplan SSSR, *Metodologicheskie ukazaniya k razrabotke gosudarstvennykh planov ekonomicheskogo i sotsial'nogo razvitiya SSSR* (Moscow: Ekonomika, 1980), pp. 754–64.

2 'On the Organization of Produce Exchange Operations with the CMEA Member Countries', a resolution of the USSR Council of Ministers of 4 August 1977, *Svod Zakonov SSSR*, no. 724, vol. 9, pp. 131–2.

3 Resolution of the USSR Council of Ministers of 9 July 1981, *SZ SSSR*, no. 652, vol. 9, pp. 54–5.

4 Decree of the USSR Supreme Soviet of 26 May 1983, and resolution of the USSR Council of Ministers of the same date, *SZ SSSR*, no. 464, vol. 9, pp. 50–1.

5 Resolution of the USSR Council of Ministers of 7 June 1984, *SZ SSSR*, no. 550, vol. 9, pp. (62–1)-63; see also O. T. Bogomolov, *Strany sotsializma v mezhdunarodnom razdelenii truda* (Moscow: Nauka, 1986), p. 250.

6 For a discussion of Gorbachev's early approaches to methods of economic administration and to the need of reform see George G. Weickhardt, 'Gorbachev's Record on Economic Reform', *Soviet Union*, 12, no. 3, 1985, pp. 251–76.

7 Gorbachev, *Perestroika*, pp. 25–6.

8 'The Key Issue of the Party's Economic Policy', report at a meeting of the CPSU Central Committee on Accelerating Scientific and Technological Progress, 11 June 1985, in M. Gorbachev, *Selected Speeches and Articles* (Moscow: Progress, 1987), p. 112.

9 B. Semenov, 'Plan i stikhiinost'', *Novyi mir*, no. 12, 1987, p. 254.

10 Martin Walker, *Guardian*, 8 February 1988, p. 8. At the beginning of October 1988, Nikolai Talyzin was re-appointed Soviet representative to Comecon, a post he had held between 1980 and 1985.

11 See 'The First Interview', *Foreign Trade*, no. 1, 1990, p. 2.
12 Ivan Ivanov, 'Gosudarstvennaya monopoliya vneshnei torgovli: formy i problemy na 70-letnem rubezhe', *Vneshnyaya torgovlya*, no. 4, 1988, pp. 2–4; 'Sovmestnye predpriyatiya – pervye itogi i perspektivy', *Kommunist*, no. 12, 1988, pp. 38–47; 'Problems of Foreign Economic Ties', *International Affairs* (Moscow), no. 11, 1988, pp. 36–40; 'Problemy khozyaistvennogo rascheta vo vneshneekonomicheskoi deyatel'nosti', *Voprosy ekonomiki*, no. 9, 1989, pp. 100–8; 'Perestroika vneshneekonomicheskikh svyazei v SSSR: pervye itogi i osnovnye problemy', *MEiMO*, no. 10, 1989, pp. 5–15; Ivan Ivanov, Aleksei Shagurin and Viktor Bossert, 'Vneshnie svyazi sovetskikh predpriyatii', *MEiMO*, no. 11, 1989, pp. 106–11; and Ivan Ivanov, 'Time to Turn Outward', *Vestnik*, April 1990, pp. 78–80.
13 Ivan Ivanov, 'From Self-Imposed Isolation to an Open Economy', *International Affairs* (Moscow), no. 4, 1989, p. 70.
14 In the late 1960s a debate resurfaced in official circles between neo-Slavophiles and Marxists that was similar to the nineteenth century debate between Russophiles and Westernizers. See 'The Struggle for Soviet Ideology: Marxists vs. Slavophiles', in Stephen F. Cohen (ed), *An End to Silence: Uncensored Opinion in the Soviet Union* (New York and London: W. W. Norton, 1982), pp. 216–22.
15 G. Sorokin, *Voprosy ekonomiki*, no. 3, 1983, pp. 131, 133; and A. Shapiro, *MEiMO*, no. 3, 1985, p. 91.
16 Andrei D. Sakharov, *Progress, Coexistence, and Intellectual Freedom*, translated by *The New York Times* (London: Andre Deutsch, 1968), p. 74.
17 F. Burlatsky, *Novyi mir*, no. 4, 1982, p. 221.
18 Yu. Shishkov, *MEiMO*, no. 8, 1984, p. 72; E. Pletnev, *MEiMO*, no. 7, 1985, p. 106. For a short description of the debate see Stephen Shenfield, *The Nuclear Predicament: Explorations in Soviet Ideology* (London: RIIA/RKP, 1987), pp. 66–9.
19 Anders Aslund, 'Gorbachev's Economic Advisors', *Soviet Economy*, no. 3, 1987, p. 259.
20 *Moscow News*, 24 April 1988, p. 5.
21 See Nikolai Shmelev, 'Avansy i dolgi', *Novyi mir*, no. 6, 1987; 'Novye trevogi', *Novyi mir*, no. 4, 1988; 'Ekonomika i zdravyi smysl', *Znamya*, July 1988, an English translation of this article can be found in Anthony Jones and William Moskoff (eds), *Perestroika and the Economy: New Thinking in Soviet Economics* (Armonk, NY: M. E. Sharpe Inc., 1989), pp. 267–76; V. Spandar'yan and N. Shmelev, 'Ob uglublenii reformy vneshneekonomicheskoi deytel'nosti', *MEiMO*, no. 9, 1989.
22 Yu. Apenchenko, 'Nedodelannye dela', *Znamya*, no. 11, 1987, p. 179.
23 Otto Latsis, 'Kak shagaet uskorenie?', *Kommunist*, no. 4, 1987, p. 61;

also Oleg Bogomolov, 'Toward Ruble Convertibility', *World Link: The Magazine of the World Economic Forum*, no. 11/12, 1989, pp. 53–4.

24 N. Shmelev, 'Avansy i dolgi', *Novyi mir*, no. 6, 1987, p. 158.

25 Mikhail Antonov, 'Idti svoim putem' *Molodaya gvardiya*, no. 1, 1988, p. 197.

26 *Ibid.*, p. 200.

27 See *Nash sovremennik*, no. 1, 1986, pp. 130–42; and no. 7, 1986, pp. 3–20; *Moskva*, no. 3, 1988, pp. 3–26. The literary monthlies *Nash sovremennik*, *Moskva* and *Molodaya gvardiya* are considered the standard-bearers of conservatism, which 'combine change-resistant politics with an unattractive streak of Russian nationalism'. See *The Economist*, 6 August 1988, p. 38.

28 'For a policy of national accord and Russian rebirth', Campaign Platform of the Bloc of Russian Public Patriotic Movements, *Literaturnaya Rossiya*, 29 December 1989, pp. 2–3, reproduced in *The Current Digest of the Soviet Press*, vol. XLII, no. 1, 7 February 1990, pp. 1, 4.

29 For example, the central Ministries of Heavy Machine-Building and of Power-Plant Machinery were abolished and a new Ministry for Heavy Transport and Power-Plant Building was created. At the beginning of 1988, 40% of officials' vehicles in the central ministries and departments were cut, while in the republics they were to be cut by 20%, the expenses of the remainder to be paid by the local organizations from their own budgets (*Der Spiegel*, no. 8, 22 February 1988, pp. 148–9). *Pravda Ukrainy* reported that nearly 80,000 bureaucrats lost their jobs in the Ukraine as part of a campaign to streamline administration. This happened when fourteen republican ministries and government agencies and 83 lower-level organizations were abolished (*The Times*, 8 February 1988, p. 7). In Estonia thirteen ministries were abolished.

30 *Pravda*, 17 January 1988, p. 3.

31 Gorbachev, *Perestroika*, p. 60.

32 See the text of the speech delivered by M. S. Gorbachev on 2 November 1987, in *Kommunist*, no. 17, November 1987, pp. 23, 26–7.

33 Resolution of the CPSU Central Committee and the USSR Council of Ministers, 'On Measures to Improve the Management of Foreign Economic Relations', in Supplement to *Foreign Trade*, no. 5, 1987, pp. 2–5.

34 See TASS in English, 6 January 1987, *SWB*, SU/W1424/A1, 16 January 1987. For a full list of enterprises, associations and organizations which changed their affiliation as a result of the enactment of resolution no. 991 of 19 August 1986, see Supplement to *Foreign Trade*, no. 4, 1987.

35 According to an official Soviet source their decision to enter into direct foreign trade transactions was to be voluntary, based on their own assessment of their potential. See Ivan Ivanov, Deputy Chairman of the State Foreign Economic Commission, speaking on Soviet television, 18 February 1987, *SWB*, SU/W1430/A/2, 27 February 1987.

36 *Ekonomicheskaya gazeta*, no. 4, January 1987.

37 Professor Igor Faminsky was nominated as the director, and its first research topic was to be the prospects of joint ventures with foreign partners. TASS in English, 12 January 1987, *SWB*, SU/W1425/A/4, 23 January 1987; see also an interview with I. P. Faminsky, 'A New Institute in the System of Foreign Economic Relations', *Foreign Trade*, no. 5, 1987, pp. 15–16. This was to be the third research institute of its type, the other two being the All-Union Market Research Institute under the Ministry of Foreign Trade, and the Research Institute of Economic and Technical Cooperation for Foreign Economic Relations.

38 See *Foreign Trade*, no. 3, 1987, pp. 2–3.

39 Resolution of the CPSU Central Committee and the USSR Council of Ministers, 'On Measures to Improve the Management of Economic, Scientific and Technical Cooperation with Socialist Countries' (19 August 1986, no. 992), in Supplement to *Foreign Trade*, no. 5, 1987, pp. 5–9.

40 Decree no. 1074 of the CPSU Central Committee and the USSR Council of Ministers of 17 September 1987, 'On Additional Measures to Improve the Country's External Economic Activity', *Ekonomicheskaya gazeta*, no. 41, 1987, pp. 18–19. The English text of the decree can be found in *Foreign Trade*, no. 12, 1987, pp. 2–6.

41 B. Dyakin, in *Planovoe khozyaistvo*, no. 1, January 1988, p. 99.

42 *Izvestiya*, 24 January 1988, p. 1.

43 Andrei Kuteinikov, 'Can Cooperatives Export?', *Moscow News*, no. 33, 27 August 1988, p. 7. The author, who criticized the conservative position of the Ministry of Finance, works at the Institute of the USA and Canada of the USSR Academy of Sciences. He noted that 'the more we resist the need for change, the greater the backwardness we will have to overcome later'.

44 *Ibid.*

45 *Ekonomika i zhizn'*, no. 12, March 1990, p. 5.

46 A report by Stepan Sitaryan, Deputy Chairman of the USSR Council of Ministers and Chairman of the State Foreign Economic Commission of the USSR Council of Ministers, in TASS in Russian, 3 April 1990, *SWB*, SU/W0123 A/1, 13 April 1990.

47 See Quentin Peel, 'The battle lines are drawn', *The Financial Times*, 20 November 1989.

48 'Man, Freedom, and the Market. On the Programme Developed by the Group led by Academician S. S. Shatalin', *Izvestiya*, 5 September 1990; also reprinted in *SWB* SU/0862 CI/1, 6 September 1990.

Chapter 3

1 *Economic Survey of Europe in 1989–1990* (New York: Economic Commission for Europe, 1990), p. 406.
2 Stephen H. Gardner, 'East-West Economic Relations: The Policy Implications of Recent Scholarship', *US-Soviet Relations*, compiled by the American Cultural Center, reprinted from a commissioned article for *Portfolio: International Economic Perspectives*, vol. 10, no. 4, p. 1. According to the Soviet Academician Oleg Bogomolov, for the 10–15 years preceding 1986 the share of the Socialist countries in world trade has been about 10%. Bogomolov (1986), p. 287.
3 Quoted in Alan H. Smith, 'Foreign Trade: Gorbachev's Inheritance', in Martin McCauley (ed), *The Soviet Union under Gorbachev* (London: Macmillan, 1987), p. 137.
4 Vladimir Treml, referring to findings by Soviet economists, estimates that in about 1980 more than 20% of capital investment in machinery and equipment in the USSR was of foreign origin, and that the share of imports was at about the same level in the total installed stock of machinery. He estimates that the chemical industry, where more than 60% of specialized machinery was of foreign origin, was particularly dependent on imports, as was the paper industry with more than 50%. See Vladimir G. Treml, 'Soviet Dependence on Foreign Trade', in *Colloquium 1983* (Brussels: NATO, Economics Directorate, 1983), p. 40.
5 B. Dyakin, 'Napravlenie korennoi perestroiki vneshneekonomicheskogo kompleksa SSSR', *Planovoe khozyaistvo*, no. 1, January 1988, p. 98.
6 See Philip Hanson, *Trade and Technology in Soviet-Western Relations* (New York: Columbia University Press, 1981), pp. 136–9, and Thane Gustafson, *Selling the Russians the Rope? Soviet Technology Policy and US Export Controls* (Santa Monica, CA: The Rand Corporation, 1981), p. 22.
7 Midland Montagu, *Tradebrief*, January 1990, p. 3.
8 See Nancy Dunne, 'Pitfalls remain along path to perfect trade relations', *The Financial Times*, 4 June 1990.
9 Ivan Ivanov, Deputy Chairman of the State Foreign Economic Commission, speaking on Soviet Television, 18 February 1987, *SWB*, SU/W1430/A/1, 27 February 1987.
10 From the report at the CPSU Central Committee Plenary Meeting of

16 June 1986, 'On the Five-Year Plan of the Economic and Social Development of the USSR for 1986–1990 and the Tasks of Party Organisations in Carrying it out', Gorbachev, *Selected Speeches*, p. 548.

11 Gorbachev, *Selected Speeches*, pp. 33–4.

12 *Ibid.*, p. 101.

13 'The Programme of the Communist Party of the Soviet Union (new edition) 1 March 1986', in *The USSR and International Economic Relations* (Moscow: Progress, 1987), p. 489.

14 Speech by Gorbachev, at an official dinner in his honour at the Elysée Palace, printed in Gorbachev, *Selected Speeches*, p. 360.

15 See John Authers, 'East European moves threaten interest rates', *The Financial Times*, 11 May 1990, p. 10.

16 According to the *International Energy Statistical Review* (CIA, Directorate of Intelligence, Washington DC, 24 April 1990, p. 1), the largest six oil producers in the world accounted in 1989 for 55% of the world total (in thousands of barrels per day):

World	*58,596*	*100%*
USSR	11,581	19.8
USA	7,619	13.0
Saudi Arabia	4,904	8.4
Iran	2,858	4.9
Iraq	2,809	4.8
China	2,765	4.7
Rest of world	26,060	44.5

17 *International Energy Statistical Review*, 24 April 1990, pp. 3, 14, 16. The USSR also imports small quantities of oil (mainly from Iraq and Libya) and gas (from Afghanistan), see *ibid.*, pp. 15, 17.

18 See Jonathan P. Stern, *Soviet Oil and Gas Exports to the West*, Joint Energy Programme, Policy Studies Institute and RIIA, Energy Papers no. 21 (London: Gower, 1987), p. 123.

19 *International Energy Statistical Review*, 24 April 1990, p. 13.

20 A report from a press conference given by B. I. Gostev on 29 March 1989, in *Argumenty i fakty*, no. 14, 8–14 April 1989, p. 1.

21 Michael Kaser, 'The energy crisis and Soviet economic prospects 1986–1990', *The World Today*, June 1986, vol. 42, no. 6, p. 91.

22 Scholars in the West predicted Soviet foreign trade difficulties stemming from changing energy prices in 1984. See for example Jochen Bethkenhagen, 'The Soviet Union in World Trade: Energy and Raw Materials' in Hans Joachim Veen (ed), *From Brezhnev to Gorbachev: Domestic Affairs and Soviet Foreign Policy* (Leamington Spa and New York: Berg and St Martin's Press, 1987), p. 68. On the

negative effect of the reduced oil price on the Soviet Union see also Christopher Wilkinson, NATO Economics Directorate, 'The Alliance and the Price of Oil', *NATO Review*, no. 1, February 1987, pp. 17–18; Alan H. Smith, 'Foreign Trade' in McCauley (ed), *The Soviet Union under Gorbachev*, 1987, pp. 135–55.

23 M. Berger, 'The Difficult Path to Recognition', *Izvestiya*, 7 August 1987.

24 *Vneshnyaya torgovlya SSSR v 1985 g.*, Finansy i statistika, Moscow, 1986, p. 6.

25 *Ibid.*, p. 16.

26 *Vneshnyaya torgovlya SSSR za 1969–1963 gody*, Vneshtorgizdat, Moscow, 1965, and subsequent annual publications of the same source up to 1986; *Vneshnyaya torgovlya SSSR v 1987 g.*, Finansy i statistika, Moscow, 1988, p. 15.

27 See 'Kim Yen Sam: perestroika nuzhna vsem', *MEiMO*, no. 6, 1990, p. 60.

28 A. Zverev, *Vneshnyaya torgovlya*, no. 9, 1986, p. 18.

29 'US, Soviet trade "set to surge"', *The Financial Times*, 11 July 1990.

30 See *The Financial Times*, 21 June 1990, p. 2.

31 *Selskaya zhizn'*, 19 May 1990, in *SWB*, SU/W0131 A/4, 8 June 1990.

32 See Viktor Shilin, 'The Aim and Problems of Increasing Machinery and Equipment Export', *Foreign Trade*, no. 3, 1990, p. 33.

33 TASS in Russian for abroad, 2 February 1990, in *SWB*, SU/W0114 A/1, 9 February 1990.

34 *Izvestiya*, 8 May 1990 (morning edition), also in *SWB*, SU/W0129 A/4, 25 May 1990.

Chapter 4

1 DeAnne Julius, *Global Companies and Public Policy: The Growing Challenge of Foreign Direct Investment* (London: Pinter/RIIA, 1990), p. 14.

2 See 'Time to Kick the Tyres', *The Economist*, 21 October 1989, pp. 108, 112.

3 See Ivanov, *Vestnik*, April 1990, p. 79; *Ekonomika i zhizn'*, no. 32, August 1990, p. 18.

4 *Vneshnie ekonomicheskie svyazi SSSR v 1989 g.*, Finansy i statistika, Moscow, 1990, p. 291. See also Appendix 6: A.6.

5 TASS in English, 12 March 1987, *SWB*, SU/W1433/A/3, 20 March 1987.

6 Carl H. McMillan, 'Soviet and East European Participation in Business Firms and Banks Established in the West: Policy Issues', *Colloquium 1983* (Brussels: NATO, Economic Directorate, 6–8 April 1983), pp. 288–90.

7 See Akademiya Vneshnei Torgovli, *Dve sistemy mirovogo khozyaistva:*

antagonisticheskoe edinstvo (Moscow, 1983), pp. 13–16, quoted in E.
Pletnev, 'Mirokhozyaistvennyi srez perestroiki i ekonomicheskaya
teoriya', *MEiMO*, no. 7, 1988, p. 87.

8 On some legal implications of the above agreements see Pavel
Smirnov, 'Joint Ventures on Soviet Territory', *Foreign Trade*, no. 1,
1988, p. 46.

9 'Skol'ko sovmestnykh predpriyatii?', *Pravda*, 16 April 1989.

10 *Vestnik*, March 1990, p. 52.

11 Decree no. 6362-XI of the Presidium of the USSR Supreme Soviet,
'On Questions Concerning the Establishment in the Territory of the
USSR and Operation of Joint Ventures, International Amalgamations
and Organizations with the Participation of Soviet Foreign
Organizations, Firms and Management Bodies', in *Documents on the
Reorganization of the USSR Foreign Economic Ties*, supplement to
Foreign Trade, no. 5, 1987, p. 10.

12 The data for 1987–8 are from Leonard Geron, *Joint Ventures in the
USSR: Data Base* (London: RIIA, 1989), and those for 1989 are from
Dmitri Kuzmin, 'Joint Ventures: the Upward Trend', *Vestnik*, March
1990, p. 52.

13 By the end of 1988, the cumulative amount of FDI pledged in China
amounted to $28.06bn for 15,942 contracts. Foreign investment in
China has slowed down, however, since the Tiananmen Square events
of June 1989 and the subsequent political crack-down on dissidents.
The data on FDI in China is from the Ministry of Foreign Economic
Relations and Trade, PRC, in Shen Xiaofang, 'A Decade of Direct
Foreign Investment in China', *Problems of Communism*, March-April
1989, p. 63.

14 DeAnne Julius and Stephen E. Thomsen, *Inward Investment and
Foreign-owned Firms in the G-5*, RIIA Discussion Paper no. 12
(London: RIIA, 1989), p. 26.

15 *Izvestiya*, 24 January 1988, p. 1.

16 See Quentin Peel, 'British Anger at Moscow Quota', *The Financial
Times*, 24 May 1989; and 'British Businesses Excluded from Soviet
Employee Quota', *The Financial Times*, 31 May 1989.

17 The sum of profit is defined as the difference between the balance of
profit and deductions to the reserve fund (which is to be deducted
from profits until it totals 25% of the authorized fund of the JV) and
other funds (necessary for its operation and for the social needs of its
personnel, which are to be specified by the foundation documents) of
the joint venture. The tax is assigned to the Union budget. See decree
no. 49, 13 January 1987.

18 *International Herald Tribune*, 8 February 1988, p. 13.

19 *The Financial Times*, 15 June 1990.

20 According to *Handbook of Economic Statistics* (Washington, DC: CIA, Directorate of Intelligence, for the appropriate year), the average annual $/rouble exchange rates for the 1980s are as follows:

1980: 1.54	1985: 1.19
1981: 1.39	1986: 1.42
1982: 1.38	1987: 1.57
1983: 1.35	1988: 1.65
1984: 1.23	1989: 1.62

21 *Barometer* (Zurich: Link, February 1990), p. 43.

22 Taken from the answers that Ryzhkov gave to a journalist of the West German magazine, *Neue Gesellschaft-Frankfurter Hefte*, 'Prospects of Economic Cooperation with Western Europe', *Foreign Trade*, no. 11, 1986, p. 4. The complete text is published in *New Times*, no. 38, 1986.

23 Complaints against the Soviet management had been voiced, for example, by both Soviet employees and the foreign partners in the case of a Soviet-British JV, Dinamika. The JV's management appears to be inconsistent and arbitrary in respect of the local labour force, as well as in respect of the JV's main functioning conditions (it was set up to develop educational programming, but after a successful initial stage turned to simple trade transactions, which are more profitable). Moreover, the Western partner (Gerald Computers) is not being consulted on major policy decisions. See 'Zachem sozdavalas' Dinamika', *Ekonomicheskaya gazeta*, no. 17, April 1989.

24 See Janice Castro, 'Joint Misadventures', *Time International*, no. 15, 10 April 1989, p. 41.

25 See, for example, Charles Leadbeater, 'Pioneer Spirit Thrives in the Wild East', *The Financial Times*, 15 June 1990.

26 Nikolai Shmelev, 'Avansy i dolgi', *Novyi Mir*, no. 6, 1987, p. 154.

27 A problem of quality and supplies arose, for example, in the case of the Soviet-Spanish JV, Telur. The JV started the production and marketing of telephones in November 1988. Some 60% of the components are Soviet, which creates two major problems for the JV: erratic deliveries from the suppliers and the low quality of some of the components. As a result, the firm is unable to operate smoothly, production has been halted (sometimes for days), and the customers complain about the quality of the product (the dialling mechanism does not work properly). See 'Telur i ego zaboty', *Ekonomicheskaya gazeta*, no. 17, April 1989.

28 *Ekonomika i zhizn'*, no. 28, July 1990.

29 See *The Financial Times*, 2 September 1987.

30 See 'Vneshneekonomicheskie svyazi SSSR v protsesse perestroiki', *MEiMO*, no. 9, 1988, p. 112.

31 See *Izvestiya*, 19 May 1990; *SWB*, SU/0782 i, 5 June 1990.

32 Abel Aganbegyan, speaking at a news conference in Moscow on 3 April 1989, quoted in *SWB*, SU/W0072 A/2-A/3, 14 April 1989.

33 Decree no. 1074, of 17 September 1987, in *Foreign Trade*, no. 12, 1987, p. 5.

34 *SWB*, SU/0808 i, 5 July 1990.

35 TASS in English, 18 April and 11 May 1990, *SWB*, SU/W0131 A/5–6; Moscow home service, 15 May 1990, in *SWB*, SU/W0129i, 25 May 1990.

36 Out of the total amount of R52m of foreign capital invested in concessionary enterprises by September 1927, R14.6m were British, R12.3m were American, and R7.1m were German (Germany's portion reflecting relatively greater technological intensity). Britain, the USA, Germany and Sweden owned 77.8% of the total capital invested in concessionary enterprises. The remaining 22.2% belonged to 13 other countries.

37 ISIC has been used for the analysis of the sectoral distribution of joint ventures in the USSR. See *Indexes to the International Standard Industrial Classification of All Economic Activities*, Statistical Papers Series M, no. 4, Rev. 2, Add 1 (New York: UN, 1971).

38 See Economic Commission for Europe, *East-West Joint Ventures: Economic, Business, Financial and Legal Aspects* (New York: UN, 1988), p. 102.

39 In 1927 the largest concessionary share in the Soviet economy was granted in the mining sector: 46.6%.

40 An illustration of the reasons for Western worries about Soviet economic and political stability is provided by the following example: AGV-Lietuva, an Italian-Lithuanian JV for the production of sports helmets, was registered in mid-1989. The Italian partner intended to obtain credits from Mediocredito Centrale bank to pay for 85% (amounting to $4.5m) of deliveries of Italian equipment and technology. However, by May 1990 it became clear that the Italian bank had refused to provide the necessary credit because of the perceived increase in financial risk in Lithuania (at that time under the Soviet economic blockade). The Italian partner was thus obliged to buy out the Lithuanian partner's share in the authorized capital and find a new partner (which in this case became the Steklovolokno association from Polotsk in Belorussia). See TASS in Russian for abroad, 22 May 1990, in *SWB*, SU/W0130 A/2, 1 June 1990.

Chapter 5

1 For a good recent survey and analysis of GATT, see John H. Jackson, *Restructuring the GATT System* (London: RIIA/Pinter, 1990).

2 'Ninth Session of the Joint Soviet-American Commercial Commission', *Foreign Trade*, no. 4, 1987, pp. 32–3.

3 See Akio Kawato, 'The Soviet Union: A Player in the World Economy?', in Tsuyoshi Hasegawa and Alex Pravda (eds), *Perestroika: Soviet Domestic and Foreign Policies* (London: RIIA/ Sage, 1990), p. 132.

4 *Pravda*, 20 May 1987 (first edition).

5 See I. Artem'ev and S. Stankovsky, 'GATT i interesy SSSR', *MEiMO*, no. 8, 1989, p. 36.

6 For example, in a publicized dispute between the US and Soviet airlines, in the spring of 1990, the Soviet side demanded that foreign airline tickets should be sold in the USSR only for hard currency. See 'A Currency Dispute Stalls US-Soviet Airline Talks', *International Herald Tribune*, 23 May 1990.

7 See Ippolit Dumulen, 'GATT and State Regulation of the USSR's Foreign Economic Ties', *Foreign Trade*, no. 1, 1990, pp. 33–4.

8 See Artem'ev and Stankovsky, 'GATT i interesy SSSR', p. 37.

9 Harald B. Malmgren, 'The Soviet Union and the GATT: Benefits and Obligations of Joining the World Trade Club', *Public Policy Papers* (New York: Institute for East-West Security Studies, 1989), p. 15. Another Western author has argued along similar lines: 'Nothing can be gained by piling on the Soviet issue, and the effort could add to the existing difficulties [of GATT]'. William Diebolt, 'The Soviet Union and GATT' in Carl Jacobsen (ed), *Soviet Foreign Policy: New Dynamics, New Themes* (Ottawa: Macmillan/CIIPS, 1989), p. 122.

10 To improve relations between the USSR and the Philippines the two countries have agreed to ensure the issue of entry visas to their respective nationals within 20 working days. *Vestnik*, April 1990, p. 12.

11 See Ed. A. Hewett, 'The Foreign Economic Factor in Perestroika', in Paul Lerner (ed), *The Soviet Union 1988: Essays from the Harriman Institute Forum* (New York: Crane Russak, 1989), p. 133.

12 In mid-1990 the quota of these individual countries was as follows: USA, 20.08%; Japan, 4.73%; China, 2.68%; UK, 6.94%; France, 5.02%; FRG, 6.06%; Saudi Arabia, 3.59%.

13 See S. V. Gorbunov, *Mezhdunarodnyi valyutnyi fond: protivorechiya kapitalisticheskogo valyutnogo regulirovaniya* (Moscow: Mezhdunarodnye otnosheniya, 1988). In this monograph the author describes the IMF as a tool in the hands of the 'imperialist powers', especially the US. He accuses the IMF of being undemocratic, inefficient, and sees it as a tool of capitalism to strengthen its position

but, 'which unavoidably lead to the sharpening of its deep contradictions'. (pp. 168–9).

14 Ivan Ivanov, *International Affairs* (Moscow), no. 4, 1989, p. 71.

15 For a brief description of the changes in this area of Soviet foreign relations, see Anders Aslund, 'The new Soviet policy towards international economic organisations', *The World Today*, February 1988, vol. 44, no. 2, pp. 27–30.

16 Guzel Anulova, 'The USSR and International Monetary Organizations', *Interfax*, 3 November 1989.

17 See Richard E. Feinberg, 'The Soviet Union and the Bretton Woods Institutions: Risk and Rewards of Membership', *Public Policy Papers* (New York: Institute for East-West Security Studies, 1989), p. 17.

18 Most of the information on MIGA, IFS and FIAS mentioned here is from Nancy Dunne, 'Easing the path to investment', *The Financial Times*, 4 June 1990, p. 26.

19 Feinberg, 'The Soviet Union and the Bretton Woods Institutions', p. 6.

20 The figure used is calculated from *Handbook of Economic Statistics 1988* (Washington, DC: C.I.A., 1988), p. 32.

21 Viktor Belkin, a senior Soviet economist, estimated that Soviet output is about one-fourth of the American output. See William Safire, 'Weighing the Soviet Economy: How the CIA Blew it', *International Herald Tribune*, 28–9 April 1990.

22 See 'Loans, gifts and promises', *Arguments and Facts International*, vol. 1, no. 1, January 1990, p. 26. The article quotes an example of how Soviet aid to its allies is sometimes ill-conceived: 'A ton of cement exported to Vietnam costs [the Vietnamese] less than a ton of sand extracted in Vietnam itself, so there is little incentive for the Vietnamese to develop their own cement industry, especially as imported cement is supplied on credits whose repayment will begin in 20 or 30 years time.'

23 *Handbook of Economic Statistics, 1989* (Washington, DC: C.I.A., September 1989), pp. 175 and 179.

24 B. Sergeev, 'Shchedra ruka dayushchego', *Ekonomika i zhizn'*, no. 12, March 1990, p. 6.

25 A senior Soviet official has expressed the view that 'nothing terrible will happen if the Soviet Union reduces its global role'. See Vitalii Zhurkin, Director of the Institute of Europe, *Izvestiya*, 26 May 1990.

26 See Peter Norman, 'BERD gets ready to fly', *The Financial Times*, 29 May 1990.

27 According to the text of the draft Articles of Agreement of the European Bank of Reconstruction and Development, 1990 – kindly

provided by the Bank of England – the following are the shares of the recipient East European countries and Yugoslavia (per cent of total):

Total	13.5
USSR	6.0
GDR	1.5
Czechoslovakia	1.3
Poland	1.3
Yugoslavia	1.3
Bulgaria	0.8
Hungary	0.8
Romania	0.5

28 See Ernest Obminsky,† 'Toppling Trade Hurdles', *Vestnik*, March 1990, pp. 38–9.
29 Ivanov, *Vestnik*, April 1990, p. 80.
30 Obminsky, 'Toppling Trade Hurdles', pp. 38–9.

Chapter 6

1 *Economic Survey of Europe in 1989–90* (New York: Economic Committee for Europe, 1990), p. 404.
2 Thus, for example, while the officials of the Soviet Union, China, North Korea and Mongolia have agreed on the delivery of 140,000 tonnes of mineral fertilizers for 1989 through one of the border crossings by rail, actual contracts were signed for the delivery to China alone of 752,338 tonnes. Because of the limited capacity of the railway line, and because of bureaucratic inefficiency, the railway system got clogged and many goods had to be sent back. See V. Sereda, 'A Major Shortcoming of Major Trade', *Gudok*, 19 April 1990, in *SWB*, SU/W0130 A/8, 1 June 1990; also *Izvestiya* (morning edition), 26 May 1990, in *SWB* SU/W0131 A/2, 8 June 1990.
3 See David Hall, 'No grit, no pearls', *Arguments and Facts International*, vol. 1, no. 3, 1990, p. 23.
4 There are about 2m people in gaol in the Soviet Union, one of the highest per capita rates in the industrial world. See Jack Chislom, 'Inside the Gulag', *The Sunday Times*, 10 June 1990, p. 3. For a detailed account of the growing crime rate in the USSR, see Yu. Yakutin, 'Volna prestupnosti narastaet', *Ekonomika i zhizn'*, no. 28, July 1990, p. 11.
5 'Gorbachev seeks foreign capital for new housing', *Daily Telegraph*, 21 May 1990.
6 N. I. Ryzhkov, 'Effectiveness, consolidation, reform – the road to healthy economy', speech delivered at the Second Congress of

People's Deputies of the USSR, reported in *Pravda*, 14 December 1989, p. 2. Some of the strikes and boycotts were triggered by inter-ethnic strife, especially in the southern republics of Azerbaijan, Armenia, Georgia, Uzbekistan and Tadjikistan.

7 L. Abalkin, 'Rynok ne terpit diletantstva', *Ekonomika i zhizn'*, no. 21, May 1990.

8 DeAnne Julius and Stephen E. Thomsen, *Foreign Direct Investment among the G-5*, RIIA Discussion Paper no. 8, (London: RIIA, 1988).

9 See DeAnne Julius, *Global Companies and Public Policy: The Growing Challenge of Foreign Direct Investment* (London: RIIA/Pinter, 1990), p. 3.

10 Quoted in Walter Schwarz, 'The dirty men of Europe', *Guardian*, 19 January 1990, p. 23.

11 See 'The sick society', *Arguments and Facts International*, vol. 1, no. 3, 1990, p. 6.

12 See 'The stolen sea', *The Sunday Times Magazine*, 4 March 1990, pp. 32–8. The average use of chemicals per hectare was some 25 times greater in Central Asia than in the rest of the USSR. Traces of Agent Orange, a defoliant notorious for its use in Vietnam, and later used to ease the harvesting of cotton in Central Asia, were found in butter sold in the Baltic States.

13 For a detailed account of the Chernobyl disaster and its consequences see Zhores Medvedev, *The Legacy of Chernobyl* (Oxford: Basil Blackwell, 1990).

14 Paul Brown, 'Three million more may flee Chernobyl', *Guardian*, 21 May 1990.

15 Medvedev, *Legacy of Chernobyl*, pp. 313–14.

16 Among the many studies on the Chinese experience, in particular see Shen Xiaofang, 'A Decade of Direct Foreign Investment in China', *Problems of Communism*, March-April 1990, p. 67.

17 As early as October 1988, Mr Ciriaco de Mita, the Italian Prime Minister, during a visit to Moscow proposed a 'Marshall Plan' for the USSR and Eastern Europe. See Michael Ellman, *The USSR in the 1990s: Struggling out of Stagnation* (London: EIU, February 1989), Special Report no. 1152, p. 96.

18 Vladimir Popov, 'Perestroika i potrebnosti sovetskoi ekonomiki vo vneshnem finansirovanii', *MEiMO*, no. 3, 1990, pp. 32, 34.

19 According to the estimate of the New York investment bank, Morgan Stanley, it will take as much as $6,000bn–$12,000bn over 20 years to improve living standards in the USSR and Eastern Europe by 20%–30%. *Independent*, 23 February 1990.

20 See J. M. C. Rollo, 'The Role of the West' in J. M. C. Rollo (ed), *The New Eastern Europe: Western Responses* (London: RIIA/Pinter, 1990), pp. 128–31.

APPENDICES

APPENDICES

Appendix 1: Biographical notes

Leonid ABALKIN (b. 1931), a Corresponding Member of the Academy of Sciences, was appointed Director of the Institute of Economics in spring 1986. In 1989 Abalkin was nominated Deputy Prime Minister in charge of economic reform.

Abel AGANBEGYAN (b. 1932), was transferred to Moscow from Novosibirsk in the summer of 1985, after he left his position as director of the Institute of Economics and Organization of Industrial Production (IEiOPP) and as editor of the outspoken economics journal *EKO*. In the summer of 1986, Aganbegyan took over the post of Academic Secretary of the Academy's Economics Department. In the autumn of 1989 he was appointed Rector of the Academy of the National Economy (ANKh) at the USSR Council of Ministers.

Aleksandr ANCHISHKIN (1933–87), after working in Gosplan and later teaching at the Moscow State University, was appointed Director of the Institute for Economic Forecasting of Scientific and Technical Progress, which was created in summer 1985. The institute was set up within the Central Economic Mathematical Institute (TsiEMI).

Georgi ARBATOV (b. 1923), educated Moscow Institute for International Relations; member CPSU 1943- ; editor of publishing house for foreign literature and periodicals (*Voprosy filosofii, Novoe vremya, Kommunist*)

1949–60; worked for CPSU CC 1964–7; Director of the Institute of the USA and Canada, USSR Academy of Sciences 1967- ; member of Central Auditing Commission of CPSU 1971–6; candidate member and member, CPSU CC 1976- .

Oleg BOGOMOLOV (b. 1927 in Moscow) has served in the Ministry of Foreign Trade, the CMEA and Gosplan. He was an official of the Central Committee of the CPSU from 1962 to 1969. He has been head of the Institute of the Economics of the World Socialist System (IEMSS) since 1969. In March 1989 he was elected to the Congress of People's Deputies.

Valentin FEDOROV (b. 1940) is Pro-Rector of the Plekhanov Economics Institute in Moscow. He is a specialist in world capitalist economy, and previously never held any party or government positions.

Ivan Dmitrievich IVANOV (b. 1934), DSc. (Econ). 1987- , Deputy Chairman of the State Foreign Economic Commission (GVK), Council of Ministers of the USSR.

Konstantin KATUSHEV (b. 1927), Party member since 1952. Graduated from the A. A. Zhdanov Polytechnical Institute in Gorky in 1951. Worked at Gorky Motor Works. In 1963–5 he was First Secretary of the Gorky City Party Committee; 1963–5, First Secretary of the Gorky City Party Committee; 1965–8, First Secretary of the Gorky Regional Party Committee; 1977–82, Deputy Chairman of the USSR Council of Ministers; 1982–6, Ambassador to Cuba; 1986–8, Chairman of the USSR State Committee for Foreign Economic Relations; January 1988, appointed Minister of Foreign Economic Relations.

Ernest OBMINSKY (b. 1931), DSc. (Econ). In 1953 graduated from the Moscow State Institute of Foreign Relations; 1969–74, staff member UNCTAD Secretariat; 1975–9, Vice Rector USSR Diplomatic Academy; 1979–83, Counsellor in Thailand; 1984–6, Deputy Director, International Workers' Movement Institute; 1986- , Chief of Directorate for International Economic Relations, Ministry of Foreign Affairs; 1990, Deputy Minister of Foreign Affairs and Ambassador Extraordinary and Plenipotentiary.

Nikolai SHMELEV, DSc. (Econ), Professor at the Institute of the USA and Canada in Moscow; in March 1989 elected by the USSR Academy of Sciences as People's Deputy to the Congress of People's Deputies.

Stepan SITARYAN (b. 1930), DSc., Academician. Graduated from the Moscow State University. Worked as a senior economist in, and was later director of, the Financial Research Institute of the USSR Ministry of Finance. Deputy Minister of Finance. Deputy Chairman, and later First Deputy Chairman, of Gosplan. At the Session of the USSR Supreme Soviet of 24 October 1989 he was nominated a Deputy Chairman of the USSR Council of Ministers, Chairman of the State Foreign Economic Commission.

Gennady SOROKIN, originally a tax official, rose to become Director of the Institute of the Economics of the World Socialist System of the USSR Academy of Sciences, from which he was forced to retire in 1969 for making ill-judged remarks on Eastern Europe. He worked in the Research Institute of the State Planning Commission and was a department head at the Institute of Economics when he wrote the article on Eastern Europe.

Tatyana ZASLAVSKAYA (b. 1927 in Kiev) came to prominence through the critical 'Novosibirsk Report' of 1983 (see *Washington Post*, 3 August 1983; *New York Herald Tribune* and *Guardian*, both 4 August 1983; *The Times*, 6 August 1983). The report was later reproduced as 'The Novosibirsk Report', in *Survey*, vol. 28, no. 1 (120), Spring 1984, pp. 88–108. She was at that time Deputy Director under Aganbegyan of the IEiOPP. Her main work is in the area of economic sociology, which she brought to the forefront of the debate in her report, and in 1988 she was named director of the new Institute of Public Opinion.

Appendix 2: Summary of legislation on foreign economic activity in the USSR*

(*a*) *19 August 1986*: Resolution no. 991, 'On Measures to Improve the Management of Foreign Economic Relations' (to come into effect on 1 January 1987; in all, 97 ministries, departments and enterprises were granted the right of direct transactions on foreign markets).

(*b*) *19 August 1986*: Resolution no. 992, 'On Measures to Improve the Management of Economic, Scientific and Technical Cooperation with Socialist Countries' (to come into effect on 1 January 1987; on the setting up of joint ventures, international amalgamations and organizations; the introduction of currency coefficients; its aim being to raise the technical standard of output and increase output volume using the international division of labour).

(*c*) *13 January 1987*: Decree no. 6362-XI, 'On Questions Concerning the Establishment in the Territory of the USSR and Operation of Joint Ventures, International Amalgamations and Organizations with the Participation of Soviet and Foreign Organizations, Firms and Management Bodies' (two-year tax exemption for joint ventures; general statements).

(*d*) *13 January 1987*: Decree no. 48, 'On the Establishment in the Territory of the USSR and Operation of Joint Ventures, International Amalgamations and Organizations of the USSR and other CMEA Member Countries' (legal regulations concerning joint ventures; disconnection from Gosplan's mandatory plan for joint ventures).

(*e*) *13 January 1987*: Decree no. 49, 'On the Establishment in the Territory of the USSR and Operation of Joint Ventures with Participation of Soviet Organizations and Firms from Capitalist and Developing Countries' (similar to no. 48, but for capitalist countries).

* For the texts of the first six documents, identified (a) to (f), see *Mekhanizm vneshneekonomicheskoi deyatel'nosti: sbornik dokumentov* (Moscow: *Pravda*, 1988); for (g), see supplement to *Vneshnaya torgovlya*, no. 2, 1989; for (h), see *Ekonomicheskaya gazeta*, no. 3, March 1989; for (j), see *Izvestiya*, 28 December 1989; for (k), see *Ekonomika i zhizn'*, no. 12, March 1990; and for (l), see *Izvestiya*, 29 June 1990. In addition, some of the texts can be found in *Foreign Trade*, the English version of *Vneshnyaya torgovlya*. All the decrees and resolutions were issued jointly by the CPSU Central Committee and the USSR Council of Ministers, except for (c), which was issued by the USSR Supreme Soviet.

(*f*) *17 September 1987*: Decision no. 1074, 'On Additional Measures to Improve the Country's External Economic Activity in the New Conditions of Economic Management' (extension of the two-year tax exemption to be counted from the date of first profits; simplification of the procedure for setting up of joint ventures; on price reform – towards rouble convertibility).

(*g*) *2 December 1988*: Decision 'On further Development of the Economic Activity of the State, Cooperative and Other Public Enterprises, Associations and Organizations' (foreign partner may hold majority share in a JV, no restriction on remuneration of employees, reduction of JV taxes [from 30% to 10%] and longer tax holiday [from 2 to 3 years] in the Far East).

(*h*) *7 March 1989*: Decision no. 203, 'On Measures of State Regulation of Foreign Economic Activity' (introduction of export licensing; JV's export/ import activity is to be limited to its own produce [export] and for its own needs [imports], unless a special permit is obtained; Soviet economic counter-measures are possible on political grounds).

(*j*) *11 December 1989*: Decision no. 1104, 'On Additional Measures for the State Regulation of Foreign Economic Activity in 1990' (introduction of wide-ranging export licensing; most of the export items to be licensed by the MFER, also the Ministry of Fisheries, Councils of Ministers of Union Republics, Soyuzstroimater'yaly).

(*k*) *6 March 1990*: Law 'On Property in the USSR', came into effect on 1 July 1990 (foreign citizens, as well as foreign companies, may be participants in JVs; JVs may be set up as joint stock companies, parnerships with or without limited liabilities; JV property to be protected by law; foreign juridical bodies may own industrial and other property for the purpose of their business).

(*l*) *June 14 1990*: Law 'On Taxes on Enterprises, Corporations and Organizations' (corporate tax law), comes into effect on 1 January 1991, with certain parts effective as of 1 July 1990 (introduction of a unified rate of tax of 45%; JVs to be taxed on a differentiated basis according to size of foreign share - JVs with less than 30% of foreign share will pay full Soviet tax, JVs with more than 30% will pay 30% tax; it will also depend on both industrial areas and geographical location).

(*m*) *24 July 1990*: Decree of the President of the USSR on the introduction of changes in foreign economic practices (on transfer from 1 January 1991 to hard currency and on world prices settlement with CMEA countries).

Appendix 3: The main provisions of the decrees of 1988 and 1989 of the USSR Council of Ministers

'On the Further Development of the External Economic Activity of State, Cooperative and Other Public Enterprises, Associations and Organizations', 2 December 1988'*

General
– It is considered necessary radically to democratize the procedure granting the right to perform export-import operations directly.
– From 1 April 1989, the right to carry out export-import operations directly shall be exercised by all enterprises, associations, producer cooperatives and other organizations whose products (work, services) are competitive on foreign markets.

Currency
– From 1 January 1991, there will be a changeover to the use of a new exchange rate in settlements for external economic transactions.
– The application of differentiated currency coefficients when expressing actual contract prices in terms of Soviet roubles will gradually be abandoned.
– Before changing to payments using the new exchange rate, 100% addition to the exchange rate of hard currency to the rouble will be applied from 1 January 1990.
– The Vnesheconombank of the USSR will be permitted to grant bank credits up to a total of R5m in foreign currency.
– The relevant state bodies are to work out and submit (by the first quarter of 1989) concrete proposals for the stage-by-stage development of the Soviet rouble's partial convertibility into foreign currencies.

Joint ventures
– The partners' shares are to be fixed by agreement between them.
– The chairman of the board or the director-general may be a foreign national.

* Based on 'Documents', *Foreign Trade*, no. 2, 1989, pp. 44–9.

– Fundamental questions of a JV's activity shall be decided by the board on the basis of unanimity of the board.

– Questions of hire and dismissal, forms and size of payment for labour, as well as material incentives in Soviet roubles for employees of a JV, shall be decided by the JV.

– Goods imported into the USSR by a JV for its production development ma,' be subject to a minimum tax or be duty-free.

– Living accommodation and other services rendered to foreign workers of a JV shall be paid for in Soviet roubles.

– The USSR Ministry of Finance may exempt from taxation for a definite period the part of profit due to the foreign partner in a JV, when repatriated abroad, or reduce the amount of the tax, unless otherwise stated in the agreement between the USSR and the relevant state. This concession will apply mainly to joint ventures manufacturing consumer goods, medical equipment and medicaments as well as science-intensive products of macroeconomic importance, and also to JVs in the Far Eastern Economic Area.

The transfer of share, insurance and audit

– The transfer of share in a JV, the insurance against risks of JVs and also auditing of their financial and economic activity shall be effected by agreement between the parties.

The Far East

– JVs in the Far Eastern Economic Area will be exempt from the payment of profit tax during the first three years from the time of notification of the declared profit.

– The profit tax for JVs set up in the Far Eastern Economic Area will be reduced to 10%.

*'On Measures of State Regulation of Foreign Economic Activity',
7 March 1989, no. 203**

General

– Participants in foreign economic activity must be registered at the USSR Ministry of Foreign Economic Relations.

– Production cooperatives (associations) can export only their own products (operations, services). They have no right to buy up goods to resell for

* Based on decree no. 203, 7 March 1989, in *Ekonomicheskaya gazeta*, no. 13, March 1989, p. 21.

export, nor can they import goods to be resold in the USSR, or provide agency services in foreign economic operations (the same applies to other participants in foreign economic activity).
– The State Foreign Economic Commission may suspend a firm's foreign economic activity in cases of actions in bad faith or in cases where the activity causes commercial or political harm to the USSR.
– Suspension of foreign economic activity may take the form of a ban on a transaction or a temporary suspension of all similar activities for a period of up to one year.

Joint ventures
– The USSR Ministry of Finance ensures the registration of JVs in the USSR Ministry of Foreign Economic Relations.
– JVs can export only their own products, operations and services. JVs can import products (operations, services) only for their own needs.
– Permission from the USSR Ministry of Foreign Economic Relations is required to provide agency services.

'On Additional Measures for the State Regulation of Foreign Economic Activity', 11 December 1989, no. 1104*

General
– In conducting all types of foreign economic activity and for export of goods, contracts may be signed only after receiving an appropriate licence.
– Licensing of the export of the following consumer goods and raw materials for their production is to be introduced by MFER for 1990: vodka and other spirits, wine-making materials, cotton, linen and woollen fabrics, leather footwear, sewn articles, knitwear, hosiery, domestic electric appliances, clocks, motor cycles, cars, carpets, linoleum, ceramic sanitary ware, light cables, synthetic and artificial fibres, raw silk, hemp fibre, large and small untanned hides, horses for meat, flour, vegetable oils, animal food fats (including butter), sugar, meat and meat products, milk and dairy products, flax fibre, natural wool, down and untreated furs.
– The Ministry of Fisheries is to licence fish and fish products (excluding fish from internal waters, except for sturgeon);
– The Council of Ministers of Union Republics will licence fish from internal waters, except for sturgeon.

* Based on decision no. 1104, 11 December 1989, in *Izvestiya*, 28 December 1989.

– In connection with the abolition of the USSR Ministry of the Construction Materials Industry, the Soyuzstroimater'yaly state association has been empowered to issue licences for export in this sphere.

– A ban is imposed on the export, through barter operations, offshore and border trade, and direct links, of foodstuffs, coal, petroleum products, timber materials, fertilisers, construction materials and sanitary ware earmarked for sale to the population in excess of the quantities stipulated for this purpose by the State Plan for Economic and Social Development of the USSR for 1990 and the above-mentioned decision no. 1104 of December 11, 1989.

Appendix 4: Tables to Chapter 3

Table 3.1 Soviet foreign trade turnover (billions of roubles/%)

	1985	1986	1987	1988	1989
Total	142.1	130.9	128.9	132.2	140.9
Socialist countries	87.0	87.5	86.3	86.3	86.9
	61.2%	66.8%	67.0%	65.3%	61.7%
of these CMEA	78.1	80.0	79.6	78.9	78.6
	55.0%	61.1%	61.8%	59.7%	55.8%
Developed capitalist countries	37.9	29.0	28.1	31.0	36.9
	26.7%	22.2%	21.8%	23.4%	26.2%
Developing countries	17.3	14.4	14.5	14.9	17.1
	12.2%	11.0%	11.2%	11.3%	12.1%

Source: *Vneshnyaya torgovlya SSSR v 1986g.*, Finansy i statistika, Moscow 1987, p. 8; *Vneshnie ekonomicheskie svyazi SSSR v 1988g.*, Finansy i statistika, Moscow, 1989, p. 8, and *idem* 1990, p. 8.

Table 3.2 Soviet exports (billions of roubles/%)

	1985	1986	1987	1988	1989
Total	72.7	68.3	68.1	67.1	68.7
Socialist countries	44.5 61.2%	45.7 66.9%	44.2 64.9%	42.9 63.9%	42.2 61.4%
of these CMEA	40.2 55.3%	42.2 61.8%	40.7 59.8%	39.0 58.1%	38.0 55.2%
Developed capitalist countries	18.6 25.6%	13.1 19.2%	14.2 20.9%	14.7 21.9%	16.4 23.8%
Developing countries	9.6 13.2%	9.6 14.1%	9.8 14.4%	9.6 14.3%	10.1 14.7%

Source: *Vneshnyaya torgovlya SSSR v 1986g.*, Finansy i statistika, Moscow 1987, p. 8; *Vneshnie ekonomicheskie svyazi SSSR v 1988g.*, Finansy i statistika, Moscow, 1989, p. 8, and *idem* 1990, p. 8.

Table 3.3 Soviet imports (billions of roubles/%)

	1985	1986	1987	1988	1989
Total	69.4	62.6	60.7	65.0	72.1
Socialist countries	42.5 61.2%	41.8 66.8%	42.1 69.4%	43.4 66.8%	44.7 61.9%
of these CMEA	37.9 54.6%	37.8 60.4%	38.9 64.1%	39.8 61.2%	40.6 56.3%
Developed capitalist countries	19.3 27.8%	15.9 25.4%	13.9 22.9%	16.3 25.1%	20.5 28.4%
Developing countries	7.6 11.0%	4.9 7.8%	4.7 7.7%	5.3 8.2%	7.0 9.7%

Source: *Vneshnyaya torgovlya SSSR v 1986g.*, Finansy i statistika, Moscow 1987, p. 8; *Vneshnie ekonomicheskie svyazi SSSR v 1988g.*, Finansy i statistika, Moscow, 1989, p. 8, and *idem* 1990, p. 8.

Table 3.4 Soviet trade turnover with developed Western countries, 1985–9 (in million roubles)

Country	1985	1986	1987	1988	1989
Total	37,876	28,962	28,058	30,986	36,890
W. Germany	7,095	5,578	4,957	5,629	6,555
Finland	4,990	3,972	3,743	3,717	3,886
Italy	3,797	3,048	3,491	3,034	3,526
Japan	3,216	3,185	2,601	3,135	3,481
USA	2,703	1,459	1,198	2,104	3,395
Britain	1,903	1,789	2,111	2,417	3,218
France	3,779	2,671	2,608	2,769	2,567
Austria	1,669	1,393	1,031	1,167	1,434
Netherlands	1,300	800	1,013	935	1,410
Switzerland	951	743	884	1,178	1,404
Belgium	1,440	1,049	1,104	1,147	1,327
Sweden	799	543	652	709	995
Australia	546	517	361	364	605
Canada	967	634	497	551	451
Other	2,539	1,581	1,807	2,130	2,636

Sources: Compiled from *Vneshnyaya torgovlya SSSR v 1986g.*, pp. 9–14; *idem* 1987g.; *Vneshnie ekonomicheskie svyazi SSSR v 1988g.*, pp. 8–14; *idem* 1989, pp. 10–15.

Note: Countries in Tables 4–7 appear according to their overall trade value in 1989 (see Tables 3.6 and 3.7).

Table 3.5 Soviet trade turnover with developed Western countries, 1985–9 (%)

Country	1985	1986	1987	1988	1989
Total	100.0	100.0	100.0	100.0	100.0
W. Germany	18.7	19.3	17.7	18.2	17.8
Finland	13.2	13.7	13.3	12.0	10.5
Italy	10.0	10.5	12.4	9.8	9.6
Japan	8.5	11.0	9.3	10.1	9.4
USA	7.1	5.0	4.3	6.8	9.2
Britain	5.0	6.2	7.5	7.8	8.7
France	10.0	9.2	9.3	8.9	7.0
Austria	4.4	4.8	3.7	3.8	3.9
Netherlands	3.4	2.8	3.6	3.0	3.8
Switzerland	2.5	2.6	3.2	3.8	3.8
Belgium	3.8	3.6	3.9	3.7	3.6
Sweden	2.1	1.9	2.3	2.3	2.7
Australia	1.4	1.8	1.3	1.2	1.6
Canada	2.6	2.2	1.8	1.8	1.2
Other	6.7	5.5	6.4	6.9	7.1

Sources: Compiled from *Vneshnyaya torgovlya SSSR v 1986g.*, pp. 9–14; *idem* 1987g.; *Vneshnie ekonomicheskie svyazi SSSR v 1988g.*, pp. 8–14; *idem* 1989, pp. 10–15.

Table 3.6 Soviet exports to Western countries, 1985–9
(in million roubles)

Country	1985	1986	1987	1988	1989
Total	18,581	13,136	14,186	14,666	16,392
W. Germany	3,992	2,720	2,327	2,397	2,478
Finland	2,299	1,594	1,707	1,529	1,759
Italy	2,468	1,580	1,804	1,691	1,920
Japan	929	980	973	1,184	1,343
USA	326	313	279	332	530
Britain	1,218	1,274	1,586	1,794	2,209
France	2,175	1,541	1,518	1,579	1,349
Austria	804	540	431	455	430
Netherlands	987	576	781	657	972
Switzerland	384	287	344	405	416
Belgium	858	627	738	771	817
Sweden	492	298	427	463	560
Australia	14	8	12	14	18
Canada	18	10	47	16	39
Other	1,617	788	1,212	1,379	1,552

Sources: Compiled from *Vneshnyaya torgovlya SSSR v 1986g.*, pp. 9–14; *idem* 1987g.; *Vneshnie ekonomicheskie svyazi SSSR v 1988g.*, pp. 8–14; *idem* 1989, pp. 10–15.

Table 3.7 Soviet imports from developed Western countries,
1985–9 (in million roubles)

Country	1985	1986	1987	1988	1989
Total	19,294	15,853	13,873	16,321	20,497
W. Germany	3,103	2,858	2,630	3,231	4,076
Finland	2,690	2,378	2,036	2,188	2,127
Italy	1,328	1,474	1,686	1,343	1,606
Japan	2,287	2,205	1,628	1,951	2,138
USA	2,377	1,146	919	1,773	2,865
Britain	685	515	524	623	1,009
France	1,604	1,130	1,090	1,190	1,218
Austria	865	852	600	712	1,005
Netherlands	314	245	232	278	439
Switzerland	567	456	540	772	988
Belgium	582	422	366	376	510
Sweden	307	245	225	246	435
Australia	532	509	348	350	587
Canada	949	624	449	535	413
Other	1,104	794	600	753	1,081

Sources: Compiled from *Vneshnyaya torgovlya SSSR v 1986g.*, pp. 9–14; *idem*
1987g.; *Vneshnie ekonomicheskie svyazi SSSR v 1988g.*, pp. 8–14; *idem* 1989,
pp. 10–15.

Table 3.8 The balance of Soviet trade with developed Western countries, 1985–9 (in million roubles)

Country	1985	1986	1987	1988	1989	Total 1985–9
Total	−713	−2,744	313	−1,655	−4,105	−8,904
W. Germany	884	−138	−303	−834	−1,598	−1,989
Finland	−391	−783	−329	−659	−368	−2,530
Italy	1,140	101	118	348	314	2,021
Japan	−1,358	−1,226	−656	−767	−795	−4,802
USA	−2,051	−834	−640	−1,441	−2,335	−7,301
Britain	533	759	1,092	1,171	1,200	4,755
France	571	411	428	389	131	1,930
Austria	−60	−312	−169	−257	−575	−1,373
Netherlands	673	310	550	379	533	2,445
Switzerland	−183	−168	−196	−367	−572	−1,486
Belgium	276	205	372	395	307	1,555
Sweden	186	53	202	217	125	783
Australia	−518	−501	−336	−336	−569	−2,260
Canada	−931	−614	−402	−519	−374	−2,840
Other	513	−6	612	626	471	2,216

Source: as Table 3.1.

Table 3.9 Soviet exports to CMEA countries, 1985–9
(in million roubles)

Country	1985	1986	1987	1988	1989
Total	40,224	42,193	40,696	39,049	37,958
East Germany	7,670	7,884	7,636	7,193	6,663
Bulgaria	6,456	6,788	6,276	6,094	6,171
Poland	6,532	6,814	6,542	6,298	5,771
Czechoslovakia	6,830	6,947	6,777	6,385	6,255
Hungary	4,577	4,678	4,600	4,484	4,188
Cuba	3,877	3,802	3,731	3,727	3,834
Romania	1,957	2,823	2,539	2,344	2,681
Vietnam	1,176	1,318	1,454	1,394	1,391
Mongolia	1,150	1,138	1,140	1,131	1,005

Sources: Compiled from: *Vneshnyaya torgovlya SSSR v 1986g.*, pp. 9–14; *idem* 1987g.; *Vneshnie ekonomicheskie svyazi SSSR v 1988g.*, Finansy i statistika, Moscow, 1989, pp. 8–14; *idem* 1989, pp. 10–15.

Table 3.10 Soviet imports from CMEA countries, 1985–9
(in million roubles)

Country	1985	1986	1987	1988	1989
Total	37,884	37,796	38,856	39,830	40,588
East Germany	7,592	7,128	7,093	7,024	7,175
Bulgaria	6,056	6,191	6,552	6,873	7,307
Poland	5,600	6,127	6,329	7,109	7,410
Czechoslovakia	6,632	6,556	6,907	6,817	6,610
Hungary	4,892	4,873	5,080	4,943	4,813
Cuba	4,140	3,800	3,827	3,837	3,867
Romania	2,303	2,415	2,347	2,431	2,489
Vietnam	283	294	319	389	520
Mongolia	387	410	401	406	397

Sources: Compiled from: *Vneshnyaya torgovlya SSSR v 1986g.*, pp. 9–14; *idem* 1987g.; *Vneshnie ekonomicheskie svyazi SSSR v 1988g.*, Finansy i statistika, Moscow, 1989, pp. 8–14; *idem* 1989, pp. 10–15.

Table 3.11 Soviet trade turnover with CMEA countries, 1985–9 (in million roubles)

Country	1985	1986	1987	1988	1989
Total	78,108	79,989	79,552	78,879	78,546
East Germany	15,262	15,012	14,729	14,218	13,838
Bulgaria	12,512	12,979	12,828	12,967	13,478
Poland	12,132	12,941	12,872	13,407	13,180
Czechoslovakia	13,462	13,503	13,684	13,202	12,865
Hungary	9,469	9,552	9,680	9,428	9,001
Cuba	8,018	7,603	7,559	7,564	7,701
Romania	4,259	5,239	4,886	4,775	5,170
Vietnam	1,459	1,613	1,773	1,782	1,911
Mongolia	1,537	1,547	1,540	1,537	1,403

Sources: Compiled from: *Vneshnyaya torgovlya SSSR v 1986g.*, pp. 9–14; *idem* 1987g.; *Vneshnie ekonomicheskie svyazi SSSR v 1988g.*, Finansy i statistika, Moscow, 1989, pp. 8–14; *idem* 1989, pp. 10–15.

Table 3.12 Soviet trade turnover with CMEA countries, 1985–9 (%) (in million roubles)

Country	1985	1986	1987	1988	1989
Total	100.0	100.0	100.0	100.0	100.0
East Germany	19.5	18.8	18.5	18.0	17.6
Bulgaria	16.0	16.2	16.1	16.4	17.2
Poland	15.5	16.2	16.2	17.0	16.8
Czechoslovakia	17.2	16.9	17.2	16.7	16.4
Hungary	12.1	11.9	12.1	12.0	11.5
Cuba	10.3	9.5	9.5	9.6	9.8
Romania	5.5	6.5	6.1	6.1	6.6
Vietnam	1.9	2.0	2.2	2.3	2.4
Mongolia	2.0	1.9	1.9	1.9	1.8

Sources: Compiled from: *Vneshnyaya torgovlya SSSR v 1986g.*, pp. 9–14; *idem* 1987g.; *Vneshnie ekonomicheskie svyazi SSSR v 1988g.*, Finansy i statistika, Moscow, 1989, pp. 8–14; *idem* 1989, pp. 10–15.

Table 3.13 The balance of Soviet trade with CMEA countries, 1985–9 (in million roubles)

Country	1985	1986	1987	1988	1989	Total 1985–9
Total	2,340	4,397	1,840	−781	−2,630	5,166
East Germany	78	756	543	169	−512	1,034
Bulgaria	400	597	−276	−779	−1,136	−1,194
Poland	932	687	213	−811	−1,639	−618
Czechoslovakia	198	391	−130	−432	−355	−328
Hungary	−315	−195	−480	−459	−625	−2,074
Cuba	−263	2	−96	−110	−33	−500
Romania	−346	408	192	−87	192	359
Vietnam	893	1,024	1,135	1,005	871	4,928
Mongolia	763	728	739	725	608	3,563

Sources: Compiled from: *Vneshnyaya torgovlya SSSR v 1986g.*, pp. 9–14; *idem* 1987g.; *Vneshnie ekonomicheskie svyazi SSSR v 1988g.*, Finansy i statistika, Moscow, 1989, pp. 8–14; *idem* 1989, pp. 10–15.

Appendix 5: Tables to Chapter 4

Table 4.1 Changes of JV legislation in the period 1987–89

January 1987	September 1987	December 1988
Permitting authority: (a) Capitalist countries— USSR Council of Ministers (b) Socialist countries—on the basis of inter-government agreements	(a) All-Union Ministries and agencies Republican Council of Ministers (b) same as (a)	State enterprises, associations and organizations with the consent of superior management body; cooperatives—permission by Republican Council of Ministers
Partner's share: (a) Capitalist countries— Soviet majority (51%) (b) Socialist countries— not limited		Foreign up to 99%
Transfer of shares Permission from USSR ministry or agency, or Republican Council of Ministers (priority to Soviet partner)		By partner's agreement to any third party
Management: Chairman of the board or director-general must be Soviet		Chairman or director-general may be a foreigner
Personnel: Majority Soviet		
Hire/fire: According to Soviet law		According to JV management
Remuneration of employees: According to Soviet standards		Not limited

(concludes opposite)

Table 4.1 (*concluded*)

January 1987	September 1987	December 1988
Taxation and Repatriation of Profits:		
(a) 30% domestic plus 20% on repatriation (= 44%)		10% plus 20% (= 28%) in the Far East
(b) Two-year tax exemption from start of operation	Two-year tax exemption from first profits	Three-year tax exemption in the Far East
Investment valuation:		
In roubles	Any currency	
Domestic credits in hard currency for exporting industries:		
Up to 4 years	Up to 8 years	
Domestic sales and purchases:		
(a) In roubles	Any currency	
(b) Through Soviet FTOs	Not limited to FTOs	
Insurance of property risks:		
By Soviet agency Ingosstrakh		Any agency
Audit:		
According to Soviet practice and by Soviet agency		Partners free to decide on how the JV is audited
Export of goods other than JVs own product and import of goods other than for JV's own needs:		
		Allowed*

Source: Mekhanzim Vneshne-ekonomicheskoi deyatel'nosti: sbornik dokumentov (Moscow: Izdatel'stvo Pravda, 1988); *Ekonomicheskaya gazeta*, no. 51, December 1988 and no. 13, March 1989.

*This was amended in March 1989 to 'special permit required'.

Table 4.2 Results of the first three hard currency auctions

	2 November 1989	21 February 1990	10 May 1990
Offers to sell	31	31	14
Offers to buy	210	123	142
Value of roubles traded (million)	8.5	9	9.8
Average R/$ rate	15.2	21	27.11

Source: *Barometer* (Zurich: Link, February 1990), p. 43; *Ekonomika i zhizn'*, no. 9, February 1990, and no. 21.

Table 4.3 Dynamics of setting up joint ventures in the USSR, 1987–90

	7/87	1/88	7/88	1/89	7/89	1/90	7/90	1/91
Total	5	23	63	191	682	1,274	1,830	2,500e
Half-yearly number of JVs registered	5	18	40	128	491	592	556	670e
Average share of foreign partner in capital (%)	47.0	34.4	38.9	39.4	42.1	49.1	50.0	52.0e

Sources: Compiled from *Ekonomicheskaya gazeta*, nos 44, 45, 46, 48, 49, 50, 51, 1988; nos 2–4, 6–9, 1989; *Pravda*, 16 April 1989; *PlanEcon Report*, vol. 6, nos 7 and 8, 21 February 1990, p. 36; Dmitri Kuzmin, 'Joint Ventures: the Upward Trend', *Vestnik*, March 1990, p. 51; *Vestnik*, April 1990, pp. 79, 80; *Ekonomika i zhizn'*, no. 32, August 1990, p. 18.

Note: figures as on first day of the month; e = estimate.

Table 4.4 Total foundation capital of JVs by country of foreign
participant on 1 January 1989 (in million roubles)

Foreign participant's country	Foundation capital	%	Number of JVs†
Total	811.5	100.0	191
Italy	135.4	16.7	13 [17]
W. Germany	119.2	14.7	26 [29]
Bulgaria	68.7	8.5	7
Yugoslavia	60.2	7.4	6
Austria	59.2	7.3	12 [15]
France	56.6	6.9	7 [8]
Finland	49.8	6.0	25 [27]
USA	44.6	5.5	11 [13]
Switzerland	43.2	5.3	11
Japan	34.1	4.2	8
Canada	27.8	3.4	6
Hungary	16.8	2.1	5 [9]
Sweden	16.0	2.0	2 [4]
Britain	9.1	1.1	9 [10]
Other*	70.8	8.7	43

Source: as Table 3.1

*Including the foundation capital of 14 JVs with more than two partners, which
account for R24.6m and which are not included in the above country breakdown;
†Figures in parentheses include JVs with more than one foreign partner.

Table 4.5 Geographical location of joint ventures in the USSR (on 1 January)

Union Republic	1989	%	1990	%
USSR	191	100.0	1,274	100.0
RSFSR	141	73.8	947	74.3
Estonia	14	7.3	91	7.1
Ukraine	9	4.7	83	6.5
Georgia	8	4.2	34	2.7
Latvia	2	1.0	30	2.4
Belorussia	3	1.6	22	1.7
Lithuania	4	2.1	13	1.0
Moldavia	2	1.0	13	1.0
Uzbekistan	2	1.0	12	0.9
Kazakhstan	1	0.5	9	0.7
Armenia	3	1.6	9	0.7
Azerbaijan	2	1.0	7	0.5
Tadjikistan	—	—	2	0.2
Kirgizia	—	—	1	0.1
Turkmenia	—	—	1	0.1

Source: *Vneshnie ekonomicheskie svyazi SSSR v 1989g.*, Finansy i statistika, Moscow, 1990, p. 290.

Table 4.6 A summary of the sectoral distribution of JVs and their capital (1 January 1989)

ISIC, capital Major division	Joint ventures		Foundation	
	no.	%	Rm	%
Total	191	100	811.5	100
1 Agriculture	7	3.7	33.5	4.1
2 Mining	1	0.5	16.9	2.1
3 Manufacturing	84	44.0	507.3	62.5
4 Electricity, gas and water	—	—	—	—
5 Construction	10	5.2	14.3	1.8
6 Trade, restaurants/hotels	16	8.4	62.5	7.7
7 Transport, communications	8	4.2	17.3	2.1
8 Business services	27	14.1	60.8	7.5
9 Community services	7	3.7	14.5	1.8
0 Computers and software*	31	16.2	84.4	10.4

Source: Compiled from *Ekonomicheskaya gazeta*, October 1988 to February 1989. A full breakdown of the sectoral distribution can be found in L. Geron, *Joint Ventures in the USSR: Data Base*, (London: RIIA, 1989), pp. 26–32.

*Computers and software are of special interest to the Soviet economy and, therefore, have been incorporated by the author as a special '0' division.

Appendix 6: Supplementary tables

A.1 Soviet foreign trade turnover (in current billion roubles)

Year	Turnover	Export	Import	Balance	Annual change %
1938	0.5	0.2	0.3	−0.1	—
1946	1.3	0.6	0.7	−0.1	—
1950	2.9	1.6	1.3	0.3	—
1955	5.8	3.1	2.7	0.4	—
1960	10.1	5.0	5.1	−0.1	—
1965	14.6	7.4	7.2	0.2	—
1970	22.1	11.5	10.6	0.9	—
1971	23.6	12.4	11.2	1.2	6.8
1972	26.0	12.7	13.3	−0.6	10.2
1973	31.3	15.8	15.5	0.3	20.4
1974	39.6	20.8	18.8	2.0	26.5
1975	50.7	24.0	26.7	−2.7	28.0
1976	56.8	28.0	28.8	−0.8	12.0
1977	63.3	33.2	30.1	3.1	11.4
1978	70.2	35.7	34.5	1.2	10.9
1979	80.3	42.4	37.9	4.5	14.4
1980	94.1	49.6	44.5	5.1	17.2
1981	109.7	57.1	52.6	4.5	16.6
1982	119.6	63.2	56.4	6.8	9.0
1983	127.5	67.9	59.6	8.3	6.6
1984	139.8	74.4	65.4	9.0	9.6
1985	142.1	72.7	69.4	3.3	1.6
1986	130.9	68.3	62.6	5.7	−7.9
1987	128.9	68.2	60.7	7.5	−1.5
1988	132.2	67.1	65.0	2.1	2.6
1989	140.9	68.7	72.1	−3.4	6.6

Source: *Vneshnyaya torgovlya SSSR*, various years.

A.2 Soviet foreign trade by country group (per cent)

Year	Socialist countries	of which CMEA	Industrialized Western countries	Developing countries
1950	81.1	57.4	15.0	3.8
1955	79.3	53.2	15.5	5.2
1960	73.2	53.0	19.0	16.0
1965	68.8	58.0	31.2	12.0
1970	65.2	55.6	21.3	13.5
1971	65.4	56.2	21.5	13.1
1972	65.5	59.6	22.6	12.9
1973	58.5	54.0	26.6	14.9
1974	54.1	48.9	31.3	14.6
1975	56.3	51.8	31.1	11.5
1976	55.6	50.8	32.9	11.5
1977	57.3	52.5	29.6	13.1
1978	59.8	55.7	28.1	12.1
1979	56.1	51.9	32.1	11.8
1980	53.7	48.6	33.6	12.7
1981	52.8	47.6	32.2	15.0
1982	54.3	49.1	31.6	14.1
1983	56.0	51.2	30.1	13.9
1984	57.5	52.1	29.3	13.2
1985	61.2	55.0	26.7	12.2
1986	66.8	61.1	22.2	11.0
1987	67.0	61.8	21.8	11.2
1988	65.3	59.7	23.4	11.3
1989	61.7	55.8	26.2	12.1

Source: *Vneshnyaya torgovlya SSSR*, various years.

A.3 Soviet aid and arms transfers to less developed countries (in million US$)

	Aid		
	Extended	Drawn	Arms deliveries
Total	47,405	20,675	207,290
1954–77	—	—	36,400
1954–78	16,610	7,610	—
1978	—	—	9,600
1979	3,805	620	15,300
1980	2,605	955	13,900
1981	855	925	14,200
1982	1,395	1,300	15,950
1983	3,185	1,645	17,100
1984	3,205	1,510	16,475
1985	3,085	1,460	13,855
1986	3,160	1,160	15,955
1987	2,240	1,240	19,240
1988	7,255	1,255	19,315

Source: *Handbook of Economic Statistics, 1989*, Directorate of Intelligence, CIA, 1989, p. 174.

A.4 Soviet economic aid to socialist countries (in million US$)*

	1954–87	1983	1984	1985	1986	1987
Total	129,704	10,576	9,717	6,770	−587	−331
E. Europe	51,363	3,522	2,632	−190	−6,718	−7,121
East Asia	13,631	1,081	1,096	1,253	1,331	1,542
N. Korea	1,421	41	55	94	6	−33
Vietnam	12,210	1,041	1,041	1,159	1,325	1,575
Other	64,710	5,973	5,989	5,707	4,800	5,248
Cambodia	685	86	87	98	128	134
Cuba	51,374	4,901	5,040	4,590	3,693	4,028
Laos	638	100	77	101	74	95
Mongolia	13,013	886	785	918	905	991

Source: As for Table A.4, p. 178

* Estimates of direct aid on a net basis and the indirect effect of price subsidies on Soviet imports and exports.

A.5 Debt owed to the Soviet Union by foreign countries (in million roubles)

Country		Debt as of 1 November 1989
Total		85,846
Socialist countries		43,806
of which:	Cuba	15,491
	Mongolia	9,543
	Vietnam	9,131
	Poland	4,955
	North Korea	2,234
	Laos	758
	Hungary	622
	Bulgaria	434
Developing countries		42,040
of which:	India	8,907
	Syria	6,743
	Iraq	3,796
	Afghanistan	3,055
	Ethiopia	2,860
	Algeria	2,519

Source: *Pravitel'stvennyi vestnik*, No. 19, 1989; *Izvestiya*, 1 March 1990, and others in *Ekonomika i zhizn'*, No. 12, March 1990.

A.6 Export and import by 1,274 JVs in the USSR in 1989 (in thousands of roubles)

	Export/import turnover	Export	Import
Total	546,469	126,460	420,009
Bulgaria	107,361	1,674	105,687
FRG	86,246	13,408	72,838
Italy	68,899	4,734	64,165
Japan	57,083	48,106	8,977
Hungary	24,531	1,750	22,781
France	19,138	4,647	14,491
Austria	17,261	1,976	15,285
Switzerland	16,629	3,046	13,583
USA	15,218	7,390	7,828
Britain	9,904	3,747	6,157
GDR	9,229	3,279	5,950
Luxembourg	9,166	8,723	443
Other	105,804	23,980	81,824

Source: Compiled from *Vneshnie ekonomicheskie svyazi SSR v 1989 g.*, Finansy i statistika, Moscow, 1990, p. 291.

EPU7